I0390451

Shape of Derivatives after financial crises

A practitioners opinion

Ankit Singh

4/29/2019

Contents

History of derivatives

Derivatives have a fascinating, 10,000-year-old history. From the ages of Babylonian rulers to medieval times, all the way to present day electronic trading, various forms of **derivatives** have had a place in humanity's financial history. Based on an agreement around an underlying asset to exchange cash or other commodities within a specified time frame, derivatives are a way to invest and hedge assets without ever actually needing to possess the asset itself.

Ancient History

In Sumer in 8000 B.C., clay tokens were baked into a spherical sort of "**envelope**" and used as a promise to a counterparty to deliver a quantity of goods by a certain date. Based on the timeframe imprinted into the envelope vessel and the tokens themselves, sellers promised to deliver the assets. This exchange essentially functioned as a sort of forward contract, which was settled once the seller delivered their goods by the date baked onto the token.

Jumping forward to Mesopotamia in the late 1700s B.C., trade and commodity security became dictated by rulers' codes, which functioned as some of the first recorded contracts. Like those by **Hammurabi of Babylon**, these contracts were actual written agreements detailing purchasing and sales between merchants and buyers on stone or clay tablets in cuneiform. Some of these contracts functioned as futures, where delivery of future grain harvests was specified prior to planting and the seller promised to deliver a quantity of grain for an agreed upon price at the time of negotiation.

Late Antiquity

Along with early recorded forwards and futures, the Greek philosopher Thales is credited with negotiating one of the first put options for an olive harvest in the 500s B.C. After predicting a large yield for the coming season, Thales negotiated with olive press owners for the right, but not the obligation, to use their presses at harvest time. He made a cash deposit and when the season did as well as he anticipated, he leased the presses and turned a profit.

The middle Ages

Forwards, futures, and options continued to evolve during the Middle Ages when entrepreneurs negotiated commercial partnerships for sea and land ventures. In these instances, one party funded the endeavor and the other party traveled the venture with the promise to bring back requested commodities. This partnership was essentially like an early form of venture capitalism with a forward contract.

Later in 13th century Italy, one of the first derivative uses between the government and its people was formed: the *monti*. *Monti* shares were supplied by cities as promises to repay debts and raise money, but shortly after their issuance, people began using *montis* as a form of currency to pay for commodities and services.
Since *monti* value rose and fell with the wealth of the cities it was issued in, it wasn't a stable currency and eventually ceased to remain significant. But this didn't matter as some of Europe's first trade markets were forming.

Medieval Europe

In the **Most Serene Republic of Venice**, markets shaped around the demands of different merchant groups. These markets functioned with over-the-counter derivatives, where trade was mainly between the buyer and seller without a formalized exchange. Eventually, these expanded into trade fairs, with one of the most well-known being in Champagne, France where "**fair letters**" were used as a line of credit between buyer and seller instead of fiat payment. Market culture moved to port cities soon thereafter.

In the 1500s, market society found its home in Antwerp, Belgium, where for the first time a building was formally constructed to house traders for business. Known as **the Bourse**, the structure held the massive trade market where sellers from around Europe sold their wares. However, unlike the direct sale markets of the past, Antwerp traders no longer purchased commodities. They instead bought and sold the rights of commodities by trading bills of exchange. This allowed merchants to eliminate the risk of transporting their goods, and it was here that a proper European financial market was established.

Feudal Japan

While financial instruments continued growing in the West, the East had established its own market in Osaka, Japan with the country's biggest commodity: rice. Harvesters throughout Japan used Osaka's markets for sale by auction, where rice vouchers were given to buyers in exchange for cash. Around 1730, the **Dojima Rice Exchange** was formally established in Osaka and allowed for rice exchange. Two ways of exchange emerged: the **shomai** market, where different grades of rice were sold at spot price and settled with rice vouchers, and the **choaimai** market, where rice was traded on books with futures based on rice grades per season. In the choaimai market, a clearinghouse settled the record books so buyers and sellers established lines of credits with the house. The clearinghouse became the intermediary for these trade payment guarantees, thus establishing what many have considered to be the very first centralized futures market.

Modern History

In the 1800s, agricultural demand in the United States required strong trading contracts so the **Chicago Board of Trade** was formed. The centralized exchange started with the use of forward contracts, and in 1865 counter-party future agreements similar to those of the choaimai rice markets were introduced. The exchange eventually traded dairy and foreign grain along with U.S. agricultural products. This greatly expanded the number of financial instruments available for derivatives trading. Today, the Chicago Board of Trade still exists as **the CME group**.

The Computer Age

The 1970s were the next spike in derivatives' popularity as option prices and hedging were better defined with the introduction of the computer. The **Chicago Board of Options** was formed to trade options with a central clearinghouse and price listing. **Trading then became electronic** in 1992, allowing for a worldwide expansion in trading derivative, security, and commodity investments. This development paved the way for property derivatives and the eventual **subprime derivative crisis** of the early 2000s.

The publishing of the Black-Scholes model (spring 1973) roughly coincides with the start of option trading at the newly opened Chicago Board Options Exchange (26 April 1973) – two events which continued to reinforce one another's importance in the years that followed. However, both option trading and efforts to mathematically model option prices are much older.

Instruments similar to today's options have been around for more than two thousand years. Their oldest documented use dates back to Ancient Greece, where Thales of Miletus (otherwise mainly known from geometry) reportedly bought rights to use olive presses, speculating that an upcoming olive harvest would be larger than expected. Option-like instruments were also traded during the 17th century Dutch tulip bubble.

The first organized option market was set up in late 17th century London, trading both puts and calls (the latter called "refusals"). In the US, option trading (though unstandardized and therefore very illiquid) dates back to the second half of 19th century.

We can assume that people trading option-like instruments in historical times might have taken efforts to understand and price them, but we can only guess how they did it, if at all.

Today

The derivative space continues to grow with block chain technology and the crypto currency space. After **Satoshi Nakamoto**'s development of Bitcoin and **Vitalik Buterin**'s subsequent creation of Ethereum, **MARKET Protocol** will bring derivative trading via a **decentralized marketplace** using the blockchain. MARKET Protocol, a decentralized derivative protocol, allows traders to gain price exposure to assets like oil, stocks, bonds, and bitcoin by using ERC20 tokens as collateral. The protocol allows traders to hedge utility tokens as well by using **smart contracts** .

Though electronic tokens now replace the ancient clay ones of humanity's past, it's easy to see how the history of derivatives has greatly shaped the current financial investment market today. From ruler contracts and oil presses to rice markets and today's blockchain trading, derivatives play an important role in the world of trade

Attraction of derivatives

Derivatives have gained a new sense of infamy recently, due to the magnitude of some trading success stories in this sector of the market. Yet not all businesses are as successful with the use of these complex instruments. Long Term Capital Management has become a famous example of extreme failure in the financial world. The hedge fund included some of the brightest players in the financial and academic worlds. The firm took complex positions, and generated impressive returns through its early inception. As the market turned in a direction the firm was not expecting, however, soon the company would find itself posting significant losses, and unable to meet many obligations. As the firm's asset base decreased, it would find itself being more and more levered. Eventually, this small hedge fund would be deemed to have too many connections with the rest of the financial industry, and was bailed out by an investment bank coalition in connection with the Federal Reserve. Following the financial crisis, JP Morgan came out as the largest bank in the United States. In 2012, just four years removed from the financial crisis, the company announced that it had lost $2 billion in a derivatives trade. The trade was originally meant to be a hedge to other positions the bank held, attempting to decrease risk. Instead, the trader responsible took such a significant position that he would be later nicknamed the London Whale. The supposed hedging trade, which took place in the credit default swaps market, was poorly executed and monitor by the bank. Eventually, JP Morgan would be forced to accept the $2 billion dollar loss (Silver Greenberg and Eavis).

How is it possible for derivatives to be the center of both significant gains and insurmountable losses? Leverage (or gearing) consists of disposing borrowed funds in some manner in the hope of deriving speculative returns that are greater than the cost of the borrowing. One way of speculating, which should not entail a great risk, would be to buy an asset at time $t = 0$ at the spot price of $S0$ in the expectation that an increased price St at time t will enable one to realize a profit. A more risky way of speculating would be to use the same funds for buying options. The purchase at time $t = 0$ of a call option on an asset gives the buyer the right to purchase the asset at a given strike price

$K_T|0$ at the future date of $t = T$. If the price of the asset rises above $K_T|0$, then the value of the call option will rise at a rate far greater than will the value the asset itself. However, if the spot price falls below $K_T|0$, then the call option may become worthless; implying a much greater loss than if the money had been invested in the asset. A put option will allow the holder to make a similar speculation that envisages a fall in the price of the asset below the level $K_T|0$ of the strike price. To clarify these matters, we may examine the circumstances at time $t = T$, which is when the options mature. Suppose that, at time t = 0, when the investment was made, the treasurer had a sum of V0 at his disposal. Then, he would be able to purchase N = V0/S0 units of the asset. At time T, when the price is S_T, his profit or loss from the speculation will be

$$\pi_T = N(S_T - S_0) = \frac{V_0}{S_0}(S_T - S_0).$$

As a proportion of the funds at his disposal, this is (S_T /S0) − 1, which is liable to be small, if S_T does not diverge greatly from S0. The treasurer might have invested, instead, in call options. At time t = 0, the price of an option in respect of one unit of the asset is $c_T|0 <$ S0. In fact, it is probable that $c_T|0$/S0 will be a small fraction. If all of the available funds were used to purchase options, and if these were be held to maturity, then, at that time, returns from the speculation could be represented as follow:

$$\pi_T = \begin{cases} \dfrac{V_0}{c_{T|0}}(S_T - K_{T|0}), & \text{if } S_T > K_{T|0}; \\ 0, & \text{if } S_T \leq K_{T|0}. \end{cases}$$

The factor V0/$c_T|0$, which would **amplify** the difference S_T −$K_T|0$ if $S_T > K_T|0$, is liable to be far greater than the factor

V0/S0, which would amplify the difference $S_T - S_0$. Therefore, if it were profitable, we would expect the speculation involving options to yield a far greater profit than the simple investment. (For a complete comparison, we should need to know the extent of the divergence of $K_{T|0}$ and S_0). On the other hand, if $S_T \leq K_{T|0}$, then all of the money invested in options would be lost whereas, in such circumstances, the losses from the simple investment would be limited.

Types of derivatives

Future

A futures contract is an agreement between two parties – a buyer and a seller – to buy or sell an asset at a specified future date and price. Each futures contract represents a specific amount of a given security or commodity. The most widely traded commodity futures contract, for example, is crude oil, which has a contract unit of 1,000 barrels. Each futures contract of corn, on the other hand, represents 5,000 bushels – or about 127 metric tons of corn

Futures contracts were originally designed to allow farmers to hedge against changes in the prices of their crops between planting and when they could be harvested and brought to market. While producers (e.g., farmers) and end users continue to use futures to hedge against risk, investors and traders of all types use futures contracts for the purpose of speculation – to profit by betting on the direction the asset will move.

While the first futures contracts focused on agricultural commodities such as livestock and grains, the market now includes contracts linked to a wide variety of assets, including precious metals (gold), industrial metals (aluminum), energy (oil), bonds (Treasury bonds) and stocks (S&P 500). These contracts are standardized agreements that trade on futures exchanges around the world, including the Chicago Mercantile Exchange (CME) and the Intercontinental Exchange (ICE) in the U.S

Some futures contracts call for physical delivery of the asset, while others are settled in cash. In general, most investors trade futures contracts to hedge risk and speculate, not to exchange physical commodities – that's the primary activity of the cash/spot market. Nearly all futures contracts are cash settled and end without the actual physical delivery of any commodity.

All futures contracts have specific expiration dates. If you don't exit your position before that date – and it's a physically settled contract, like corn – you have to deliver the physical commodity (if you're in a short position) or take delivery (if you're long). The following image shows an example of the various monthly corn contracts available on the CME. Note that the nearer the contract expiration, the greater the trading volume – and the further out the contract, the higher the price. Some contracts – such as those based on stock indexes – are always settled in cash because there would be nothing physical to deliver. It's estimated that only 2% of all futures contracts are actually delivered. That's because most traders don't want to store, insure and deliver such a huge amount of a commodity (plus they'd have no use for it). Instead, most contracts are settled in cash – meaning, the position is closed at some point for expiration.

A contract month is the month during which a futures contract expires. Some contracts trade every month, while others trade only certain months of the year. Each contract month is represented by a single letter:

Month	Code	Month	Code
January	F	July	N
February	G	August	Q

March	H	September	U
April	J	October	V
May	K	November	X
June	M	December	Z

To avoid confusion, a contract name always includes the ticker symbol, followed by the contract month and two-digit year. The complete contract name for the December 2017 corn futures contract, for example, would be "ZCZ17":

ymbol	Contract Month	Year
ZC	Z	2017
ZCZ17		

How Futures Differ from Other Financial Instruments

Futures differ in several ways from many other financial instruments. For starters, the value of a futures contract is determined by the movement of something else – the futures contract itself has no inherent value. Secondly, futures have a finite life. Unlike stocks, which can stay in existence forever (theoretically), a futures contract has a set expiration date, after which the contract ceases to exist. This means that when trading futures, market direction and timing are vitally important.

You'll usually have some choices when choosing how long you want to make a wager for. For instance, there might be futures contracts on corn with expiration dates spaced every couple months for the next year and a half (i.e.,

December 2017, March 2018, May 2018, July 2018, September 2018 and December 2018). While it might be obvious that the longest contract gives you the most time for your opinion to be right, this extra time comes at a cost. Longer-dated futures contracts will usually be more expensive than shorter-dated contracts. Longer-dated contracts can sometimes be illiquid as well, further increasing your cost to buy and sell.

A third difference is that in addition to making outright wagers on the direction of the market, many futures traders employ more sophisticated trades – such as spreads – the outcomes of which depend upon the relationship of different contracts . Perhaps the most important difference, however, between futures and most other financial instruments available to individual investors involves the use of leverage. (For related reading, see *Futures Fundamentals*.)

here are several different types of spreads, including:

- Calendar Spreads. This involves simultaneously buying and selling two contracts of the same type and price, but with different delivery dates. These spreads are popular in the grain markets due to the seasonality of planting and harvesting. For example, you could sell the July contract for corn and at the same time buy the December contract.

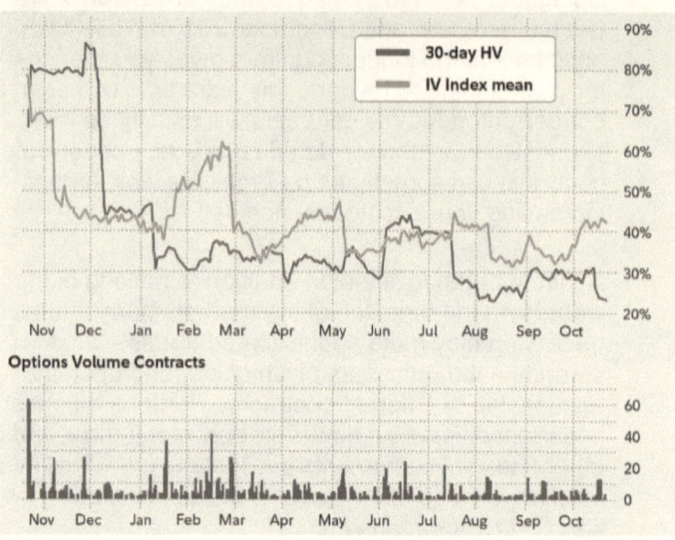

Options Volume Contracts

The profit/loss diagram of a calendar spread shows that when the stock price increases, this type of trade suffers. Significant movement in either direction in a short period may be costly because of the way the higher gamma (the rate of change, or sensitivity, to a price change in the underlying security for delta) affects short-term contracts. Another risk to this position is early assignment when selling shorter-term contracts (especially with calls), where the expiration date follows the ex-dividend date. If this is the case, the probability of assignment increases significantly. If assignment occurs prior to the ex-dividend date, the client will owe the dividend payment because the account is now short shares, unless shares of the underlying security are already held in the account. Early assignment also changes the strategy from a calendar spread to a synthetic long put if you don't already own shares, because you are short a stock and long a call, which is a very different outlook.

Managing a calendar spread

It is also advisable to check for ex-dividend dates, as it is very important to understand assignment risk—especially for call spreads. You can adjust the spread as necessary to maintain the long position, while adjusting the strike price of the short contract along the way to give more delta exposure.

Assuming a trader is considering a long calendar spread, there are traditionally two types of criteria used when filtering for such opportunities. The first is that a trader is expecting a particular underlying, or the market in general, to remain relatively tranquil during the expiration period of the short option (the nearer-term expiration).

This leg of the spread produces its maximum profit when the underlying expires exactly on the strike of the short option. The theoretical P/L of a calendar spread declines as the underlying moves farther and farther away from the short strike.

When searching for long calendar spread opportunities, traders also look for places in which implied volatility is higher in the shorter-dated expiration period, as compared to the longer-dated expiration period.

Obviously, the longer-dated option will cost more than the shorter-dated option (in terms of absolute premium) because of the extra time value in the longer dated option. However, as it relates to implied volatility in calendar spreads - it's usually preferable to sell higher implied volatility, while purchasing lower implied volatility.

For long calendar spreads, the maximum loss is the net debit of the spread times the option multiplier (100) and the number of contracts traded. The maximum loss for short calendar spreads is theoretically unlimited due to the naked short premium exposure that can exist after the near-term options expire - a big reason why short calendars are executed more rarely.

the general intent of a double calendar spread is very similar to a regular calendar spread. To deploy such a position, a trader would likely be expecting relative tranquility in the underlying over the near-term, and increasing volatility in the same underlying over the medium or longer-term.

A big difference is that the double calendar spread effectively increases the magnitude of the exposure on both legs of the spread.

Structurally, a double calendar spread involves turning your original single option spread (across two expiration periods) into a strangle or straddle (also across two expiration periods).

That means that a single calendar spread involves the deployment of a call OR a put in each expiration month, whereas a double calendar spread involves the deployment of a call AND a put in each expiration month.

Effectively, a double calendar spread, therefore, involves a straddle or strangle (one long and one short), deployed across two expiration months.

An example of a long double calendar spread is as follows:

1. Sell 10 XYZ May 40 strike calls
2. Sell 10 XYZ May 30 strike puts
3. Purchase 10 XYZ July 40 strike calls
4. Purchase 10 XYZ July 30 strike puts

As you can see from the above example, the structure of this position is effectively short the 30-40 strangle in May, versus being long the 30-40 strangle in July. Removing one of the strikes from both expiration months in this example would turn this position into a regular calendar spread.

As you might imagine, the addition of the second strike in both expiration months alters the profile of the theoretical P/L for double calendar spreads (as compared to single calendar spreads). However, the maximum loss remains the total amount paid for the spread.

The optimal outcome for a double calendar is for the short options to expire with the underlying right on the strike, or as close as possible. If you deploy a double calendar spread in strangle fashion, then the space between the strikes also represents a profit (though less than the endpoints).

Depicted below are the basic theoretical P/L profiles for a regular long calendar spread and a double long calendar spread (both theoretically traded delta neutral). These graphics should help you better understand the risk exposure represented by such trades

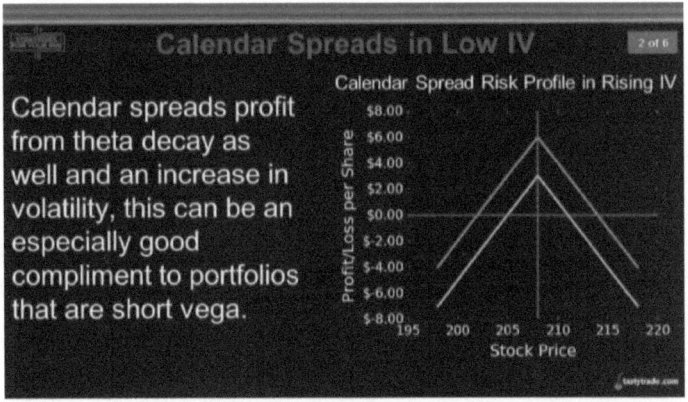

Primarily, a trader deploying a double calendar spread would be expecting the underlying to remain within the range of strikes (strangle), or near the single strike (straddle), during the expiration period which encompasses the short options. Secondarily, the trader might also expect implied volatility to increase in the longer-dated options.

Given the dynamics of the financial markets, such conditions could present themselves at any time. However, there are two trading environments/situations that traders may want to specifically monitor for calendar spread opportunities.

During earnings season, implied volatility across different expiration months can become disjointed, possibly allowing for the deployment of such a position. This may occur before or after the actual earnings announcement. Make sure you understand and accept the risks associated with trading earnings prior to adding positions like these to your portfolio.

Recent volatility in the financial markets also reminds us that another set of conditions may present themselves which could make calendar spreads attractive.

For example, imagine that the VIX has spiked (as seen in early February 2018) and that implied volatility in the near-term has increased across the board. Next, consider that earnings season is on the horizon - maybe 1 or 2 months away.

In this case, a trader could hypothetically deploy a long calendar spread (single or double) which allows them to sell higher levels of near-term implied volatility which doesn't include earnings, in favor of purchasing longer-dated premium which does include earnings.

Obviously, an integral component of such a position is that one expects near-term volatility to decrease. If one expects choppy markets in the near-term, this structure becomes less attractive, even if the earnings months is "cheaper" from an absolute implied volatility standpoint.

If you do decide to deploy an earning's related position, it's important to confirm the date of an earnings release prior to trade execution - to ensure your long position does, in fact, capture the event.

Calendar spreads offer traders a great avenue for expressing a particular market opinion. If you decide that a double calendar spread fits your outlook and risk profile, most trading platforms should allow you to deploy all four legs of the spread simultaneously.

If you can't deploy all four legs at once, it's probably best to execute the spread in two legs - a call side calendar, and a put side calendar - which in sum will equate to the double calendar.

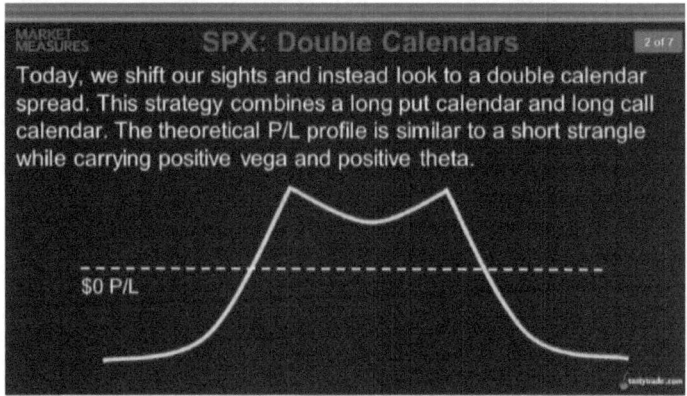

Today, we shift our sights and instead look to a double calendar spread. This strategy combines a long put calendar and long call calendar. The theoretical P/L profile is similar to a short strangle while carrying positive vega and positive theta.

$0 P/L

Intermarket Spreads. With this type of spread, you buy and sell different but often related contracts, usually with the same expiration month. You could trade an intermarket spread, for example, by simultaneously buying hard red winter wheat and selling soft red winter wheat (or vice versa, depending on market conditions). These are also called inter-commodity spreads. Another choice might include an intermarket spread. That's the simultaneous buying and selling of different, but often related, futures contracts, usually in the same expiration month, sometimes on different exchanges. Intermarket spreads are designed to capitalize on the changes in relationships between the two contracts.

For example, a common relationship exists among U.S. Treasuries' various maturities. This relationship forms the basis of the Treasury yield curve—the shape of which either steepens or flattens depending on investors' perceptions of the economy.

The yield curve steepens when the yields on bonds with longer-dated maturities rise faster than yields on shorter-dated maturities. Likewise, the yield curve flattens when yields on long-term bonds fall faster than short-term bond yields. That shift in the yield curve can be isolated through the buying and selling of the corresponding Treasury futures.

Intermarket spreads often require using a different ratio of contracts to be bought or sold.

IMPLIED TREASURY & MAC SWAP SPREADS—BASED ON JUNE 2019 FUTURES CONTRACTS				
Spread Name	Futures Contract Legs	Price Ratio*	Leg Quantity Ratio*	External Name*
TYT	2-Year T- Note vs. 3-Year T-Note	1.6667 **	5:3	TYT 05-03 M9**
TFY	2-Year T- Note vs. 5-Year T-Note	2.0000**	1:1	TFY 01-01 M9**
TUF	2-Year T- Note vs. 5-Year T-Note	2.5000**	5:4	TUF 05-04 M9**
TAF	2-Year T- Note vs. 5-Year T-Note	3.0000**	3:2	TAF 03-02 M9**
TUT	2-Year T-Note vs. 10-Year T-Note	4.0000**	2:1	TUT 02-01 M9**
TUX	2-Year T- Note vs. Ultra 10-Year T-Note	6.0000**	3:1	TUX 03-01 M9**
TUB	2-Year T-Note vs. T-Bond	10.0000**	5:1	TUB 05-01 M9**
TUL	2-Year T-Note vs. Ultra T-Bond	16.0000 **	8:1	TUL 08-01 M9**
TOF	3-Year T-Note vs. 5-Year T-Note	1.5556 **	7:9	TOF 07-09 M9**
TUN	3-Year T-Note vs. 10-Year T-Note	2.5000**	5:4	TUN 05-04 M9**
TYX	3-Year T-Note vs. Ultra 10-Year T-Note	4.0000**	2:1	TYX 02-01 M9**
TOB	3-Year T-Note vs. T-Bond	6.0000**	3:1	TOB 03-01 M9**
TOU	3-Year T-Note vs. Ultra T-Bond	9.0000**	9:2	TOU 09-02 M9**
FIT	5-Year T-Note vs. 10-Year T-Note	1.6667	5:3	FIT 05-03 M9
FYN	5-Year T-Note vs. 10-Year T-Note	1.0000	1:1	FYN 01-01 M9
FYT	5-Year T-Note vs. 10-Year T-Note	1.5000	3:2	FYT 03-02 M9
FIX	5-Year T- Note vs. Ultra 10-Year T-Note	2.5000	5:2	FIX 05-02 M9
FOB	5-Year T-Note vs. T-Bond	4.0000	4:1	FOB 04-01 M9
FOL	5-Year T-Note vs. Ultra T-Bond	6.0000	6:1	FOL 06-01 M9
NON	10-Year T-Note vs. Ultra 10-Year T-Note	1.0000	1:1	NON 01-01 M9
TEX	10-Year T-Note vs. Ultra 10-Year T-Note	1.5000	3:2	TEX 03-02 M9
NBY	10-Year T-Note vs. T-Bond	1.0000	1:1	NBY 01-01 M9
NOB	10-Year T-Note vs. T-Bond	2.5000	5:2	NOB 05-02 M9
NIB	10-Year T-Note vs. T-Bond	3.0000	3:1	NIB 03-01 M9
NOL	10-Year T-Note vs. Ultra T-Bond	4.0000	4:1	NOL 04-01 M9
NCB	Ultra 10-Year T-Note vs. T-Bond	1.6667	5:3	NCB 05-03 M9
NUB	Ultra 10-Year T-Note vs. Ultra T-Bond	2.5000	5:2	NUB 05-02 M9
BOB	T-Bond vs. Ultra T-Bond	1.5000	3:2	BOB 03-02 M9
BUB	T-Bond vs. Ultra T-Bond	1.0000	1:1	BUB 01-01 M9
FNU	5-Year MAC Swap vs. 10-Year MAC Swap	2.0000	2:1	FNU 02-01 M9

*Leg quantity and price ratios are subject to change. Highlighted ratios are unchanged from prior quarterly expiration. **Price ratios of spreads involving 2-Year and 3-Year T-Notes are doubled to account for larger notional size ($200K) in the price changes of the spreads. However, the ratio of the TYT is not doubled because the contracts have the same notional size.

- Inter-Exchange Spreads. This is any type of spread in which each position is created in a different futures exchange. For example, you may buy one contract on CBOT and sell one on NYMEX. Inter-Exchange Spreads A less commonly known method of creating spreads is via the use of contracts in similar markets, but on different exchanges. These spreads can be calendar spreads using different months, or they can be spreads in which the same month is used. An example of using the same month might be Long December Eurobund and Short December US T-bonds. Intramarket spreads will be part of the initial delivery and Inter-commodity spreads will be part of rollout. We will not cover Inter-Exchange Spreads. The most common spread type traded is the Intramarket spread, also known as the Delivery spread. An Intramarket spread position attempts to take advantage of the price difference between two delivery months of a single futures market when the trader perceives the difference to be abnormal. The Inter-commodity spreads, or trading one market against another is commonly done, and can theoretically include any commodity. However, only a few of the combinations of intercommodity spreads are exchange-recognized and receive a break in margins, as usually margins for spreads are lower. The most widely recognized Intercommodity spreads are as follows:

Grains	Petroleum	Financial	Metals	Currency	Livestock
Corn/Wheat	CrudeOil/ Gasoline	10YrNotes/ 30Yr Bonds	Gold/ Platinum	Euro/Pound Canadian/Aussy	Live Cattle/ Lean Hog
Soybeans/Soymeal	HeatingOil/ Gasoline	10 Yr Notes/ 5 Yr Notes	Gold/Silver	Yen/Pound	Live Cattle/ Feeder Hog
Soybeans/Soyoil				Euro/Swiss	

The main reasons most professional traders state for trading spreads are:

1. Lower risk

2. Attractive margin rates

3. Increased predictability

Because of their hedged nature, spreads generally are less risky than outright futures positions. Most of the professional traders who trade spreads usually cite this as their No. 1 reason. Since the prices of two different futures contracts (on the same commodity or different but related commodities) exhibit a strong tendency to move up or down together, spread trading offers protection against losses that arise from unexpected or extreme price volatility. Of course, not all spreads have lower volatility than outright futures positions, but most do—as a spread position is hedged by a long contract and a short contract, or partially "hedged". Spreads offer "protection" because losses on one side of the spread are more or less offset by gains from the other side of the spread. For example, if the short (sell side) of a spread results in a loss due to an increase in price, the long (buy side) of the spread should produce a profit offsetting much (if not all) of the loss. Because of the partially hedged nature of spread positions, spread margins tend to be margined at lower rate than outright futures positions. This is not always the case, but one can expect spread margins to be lower than outright futures positions as general rule of thumb. Like any other margin requirement, spread margin minimum levels are set by the exchange. Due to the generally lower margin levels charged for spread, traders are able to trade a large variety of positions, increasing their diversity. Also, because of the lower margin rates, which are function of volatility, spreads allow traders to risk a smaller percentage of their capital on any one trade, enabling lower capitalized traders to practice conservative money management like the commodity funds are supposed toMany spread traders feel that spreads are more predictable than outright futures positions. Some of this predictability could be due to lower risk involved in spreads-evidenced by the lower margin rates. With lower volatility, it is easier for the traders to take advantage of longer-term price moves. The lower volatility makes it easier for most traders to ride out corrections within major trends, instead of being shaken out of a position on these corrections, which often happens to straight futures traders. Also spreads are much less sensitive to sudden shocks to a market, such as news event or such. Because of this many traders feel they are more predictable. Lastly, some feel the spread markets are more predictable because they are off the beaten path. Thousands of systems have been developed for trading futures. As such, some of the strong tendencies of the market have shifted, because they have become so popular and well known. However, spread trading is still considered much too complicated or esoteric for many, and many of these spread market anomalies have not yet been worked out the market.

Leverage

In general, futures trading is considered riskier than buying and selling stocks, primarily because of the leverage involved. Leverage allows you to enter a futures position that's worth much more than you are required to pay upfront. Futures positions are highly leveraged because the initial margins (the required down payments on futures contracts) set by the exchanges are relatively small compared to the cash value of the contracts – which is part of the reason why the futures market is so popular. (Leverage is always represented as a ratio; for example, if you have access to 20:1 leverage and you have $1,000 in your account, you could enter a position worth 20 times that amount, or $20,000. The smaller the margin requirement in relation to the value of the futures contract, the higher the leverage.

With leverage, if prices up or down even slightly, the changes to your gains and losses will be large in comparison to the initial margin. Say you buy an e-mini S&P 500 (ES) stock index futures contract that's trading at 2,600, with a margin deposit of $5,000. The value of that contract is $50 times the S&P 500 Index, or $130,000 in this example – and for every point gain or loss, you stand to gain or lose $50.

Assume the ES rallies to 2,700 – for a gain of $5,000 (100 points X $50). Not bad for your initial $5,000 investment.

But before you get too excited, consider what happens if the ES drops the same amount in the other direction – to 2,500. In that case, you would have lost $5,000 (your entire investment). Even a small downward shift in price can lead to big losses with this leverage.

While leverage makes it possible to trade larger positions, it's important to remember that leverage magnifies both profits and losses.

Forward

A *forward* in the world of corporate finance is an agreement between parties to perform a sale of a specific type of good in a predetermined quantity at a predetermined price at a predetermined date in the future.

Unlike options, which give either the buyer or the seller the right to participate in the transaction but do not obligate them, forward contracts are legal obligations to perform the transaction on or before a specific date. The good thing about forwards is that they're very customizable and can include any details or additional terms as long as all the relevant parties agree to the terms.

Say that Janna wants to buy 200.5 pounds of wool. The industry standard is to sell wool only by the pound, not divisions of a pound. Janna is afraid that the price is going to increase before this season's *cuttings* (the wool term for *crop*), so she goes and talks to the farmer who produces the wool.

Janna and the farmer agree to a forward contract because the farmer is afraid that the price may drop. These are the terms of their contract:

Product: White lamb's wool, first cutting of the season, carded

Quantity: 200.5 pounds

Delivery Price: $1,500

Delivery Date: February 28, 2013

Both parties in the contract must execute their part in the contract, and the contract itself is likely to include penalties for nondelivery. Note that in the preceding example, the quantity agreed upon is 200.5 pounds, despite the industry standard of selling in increments of 1 pound. This high customizability is one of the primary benefits of a forward contract.

RISK MANAGEMENT AND FORWARD CONTRACTS

The reason companies and individuals enter into forward contracts is to reduce the amount of price uncertainty and volatility, particularly seasonal volatility, involved with buying or selling goods. Forward contracts allow buyers and sellers to agree upon a price and quantity of goods to be exchanged, sometimes even before production has begun.

For buyers, not only does this arrangement provide increased certainty that they'll get exactly the quantity they need without competing with other buyers for the same pool of suppliers, but it also guarantees that the price won't increase by the time of the delivery date.

For sellers, forward contracts not only ensure that they'll have a buyer for their products rather than risking being left with a surplus but also guarantees that the price won't drop suddenly before the delivery date.

On both a national scale and a global scale, the use of derivatives in managing risk means price stability. Many goods around the world, particularly primary goods such as agriculture, experience seasonal fluctuations. During harvest season, the quantity of goods supplied increases quite a lot, while during the off-season, the quantity drops below demand.

These fluctuations in supply cause serious seasonal price volatility. Derivatives in general help alleviate this volatility, and forwards are easily the best method for addressing the individual needs of both buyers and sellers.

REVENUE GENERATION WITH FORWARD CONTRACTS

Generating revenues with forward contracts is somewhat more difficult than doing so with most other forms of derivatives. Because forward contracts are so customizable, they aren't conducive to trading. After all, finding another buyer who wants the exact same contract you created to fit your needs and those of the other party can be nearly impossible.

s a buyer, you can enter into a contract that has a price very low compared to your estimate of the future market price (also called the *spot rate*), get your inventory of goods, and then resell them at the market price. If you're a seller, you can simply enter into a contract that has a price much higher than your expected future market price.

VALUATION OF A FORWARD CONTRACT

The value of a forward contract depends greatly on the fluctuations in the market price of goods. You can use a number of different calculations to determine the value of a forward contract, but generally speaking, each calculation is built on the following two basic ideas:

- The current price of a forward contract should be equal to the market price of goods at the delivery date plus the opportunity cost associated with not pursuing the next best opportunity. For example, if you're an investor, then the price of the forward contract today should be equal to the market price at the date of delivery plus the market rate of compounding interest.

Of course, you can't know exactly what the future market price will be (if you could, forward contracts wouldn't serve much purpose). That degree of uncertainty is where people attempt to generate income by speculating.

- At the time of delivery, the value of the forward rate is equal to the delivery price minus the market price. This is a rather simple hindsight measure that determines how effective you were at utilizing forward contracts.

In the context of foreign exchange, forward contracts enable you to buy or sell currency at a future date. Then again, all foreign exchange derivatives do the same. There are differences among foreign exchange derivatives in terms of their characteristics. Forward contracts have the following characteristics:

- Commercial banks provide forward contracts.

- Forward contracts are not-standardized. This characteristic indicates that you can have a forward contract for any amount of money, such as buying €154,280.72 (as opposed to being able to buy only in multiples of €100,000).

- Forward contracts imply an obligation to buy or sell currency at the specified exchange rate, at the specified time, and in the specified amount, as indicated in the contract.

- Forward contracts are not tradable.

Who would use forward contracts? The non-standardized and obligatory characteristics of forward contracts work well for export–import firms because they deal with any specific amount of account receivables or payables in foreign currency. Additionally, these firms know their account receivables and payables in advance, so a binding contract isn't a problem.

Take a look at the following two examples, to get some insight:

- Suppose that you're an American importer, and you have to pay €109,735.04 to a German exporter on November 12, 2012. You get a forward contract today to buy €109,735.04 at the dollar–euro exchange rate of $1.10 on November 12, 2012. In this case, you're contractually obligated to buy €109,735.04 on November 12, 2012. On this date, you will pay $120,708.54 for it (€109,735.04 x 1.10).

- Or suppose that you're an American exporter, and you expect euro-receivables on November 12, 2012. Because an American firm cannot use euros in its daily operations, as soon as you receive euros, you sell them in exchange for dollars.

  Therefore, you get a forward contract to sell euros. Suppose that your firms' receivables amount to €246,947.40, and you get a forward contract today to sell €246,947.40 at the dollar–euro exchange rate of $1.10 on November 12, 2012. In this case, you will receive $271,642.14 on November 12, 2012 (€246,947.40 x $1.10).

Forward contracts aren't tradable. This characteristic along with their non-standardized nature makes forward contracts unattractive to speculators.

Options

Options are a financial derivative sold by an option writer to an option buyer. They are typically purchased through online or retail brokers. The contract offers the buyer the right, but not the obligation, to buy (call option) or sell (put option) the underlying asset at an agreed-upon price during a certain period of time or on a specific date. The agreed upon price is called the strike price. American options can be exercised any time before the expiration date of the option, while European options can only be exercised on the expiration date (exercise date). Exercising means utilizing the right to buy or the sell the underlying security. Call Option

Call options provide the option buyer with the right to buy an underlying security at the strike price, so the buyer wants the stock to go up. Conversely, the option writer needs to give the underlying security to the option buyer, at the strike price, in the event that the stock's market price exceeds the strike price.

An option writer who sells a call option believes that the underlying stock's price will drop or stay the same relative to the option's strike price during the life of the option, as that is how they will reap maximum profit. The writer's maximum profit is the premium received when selling the option.

If the buyer is right, and the stock rises above the strike price, the buyer will be able to acquire the stock for a lower price (strike price) and then sell it for a profit at the current market price. However, if the underlying stock is not above the strike price on the expiration date, the option buyer loses the premium paid for the call option.

Risk to the call buyer is limited to the premium paid for the option, no matter how much the underlying stock moves. The profit at expiration, if applicable, is: Current market price of Underlying – (Strike Price + Premium paid) = Profit. This would be multiplied by the number of contracts and then multiped by 100 (assuming each contract represents 100 shares. This will give the total profit or loss to the trader in dollars.

The risk to the call writer is much greater. Their maximum profit is the premium received, but they face infinite risk because the stock price could continue to rise against them. To offset this risk, many option writers use covered calls.

Put Option

Put options give the option buyer the right to sell at the strike price, so the put buyer wants the stock to go down. The opposite is true for a put option writer. For example, a put option buyer is bearish on the underlying stock and believes its market price will fall below the specified strike price on or before a specified date. On the other hand, an option writer who writes a put option believes the underlying stock's price will stay the same or increase over the life of the option.

If the underlying stock's price closes above the specified strike price on the expiration date, the put option writer's maximum profit is achieved. They get to keep the entire premium received.

Conversely, a put option holder benefits from a fall in the underlying stock's price below the strike price. If the underlying stock's price falls below the strike price, the put option writer is obligated to purchase shares of the underlying stock at the strike price. The put option buyer's profit, if applicable, is calculated by taking the Strike Price – (Current market price + Premium paid). This is then multiplied by 100 (if each contract is 100 shares) and the number of contracts bought.

The risk to the option writer if the stock price falls is that they have to buy the stock at the strike price. Some traders write put options at strike prices where they want to buy stock anyway. If the price falls to that price, they buy the stock because the option buyer will exercise the option. They get the stock at the price they want, with the added benefit of receiving the option premium.

Real World Example of an Option

Suppose that Microsoft shares are trading at $108.00 per share and you believe that they are going to increase in value. While you could simply buy the stock, you want greater earning potential without the use of margin, or borrowed funds.

Call options provide a great alternative way to speculation on this increase in price. You decide to purchase one call option with a strike price of $115.00 for one month in the future for $0.37 per contact. Your total cash outlay is $37.00 for the position, plus fees and commissions.

If the stock rises to $116.00, your option will be worth $1.00, since you could exercise the option to acquire the stock for $115.00 and immediately resell it for $116.00. The profit on the option position would be 170.3% since you paid $0.37 and earned $1.00—that's much higher than the 7.4% increase in the underlying stock price.

If the stock fell to $100.00, your option would expire worthless and you would be out $37.00. The upside is that you didn't have to buy 100 shares, which would have resulted in a $8 per share, or $800, total loss. Options can help limit your downside There are 2 broad categories of stock options in option trading; Standardized Options and Non-Standardized Options. Standardized Options, or sometimes known as "Plain-Vanilla Options", are the typical call options and put options traded over the stock exchanges. Standardized Options are the most commonly traded form of options and is what everyone is referring to when talking about call options and put options in options trading.

Non-Standardized Options are options that comes with special conditions, making them more flexible and better suited for individual investor needs.

As the additional conditions in Non-Standardized Options can be highly complex, they are not normally traded over the stock exchanges for the purpose of option trading. This kind of non-standardized options are known as Exotic Options. Exotic options are more commonly traded in the currency market than in the stock market.

Exotic options are also slowly moving out of the OTC market and into the public exchanges as they gain in standardization and popularity. Since 2008, Binary Options has been approved for listing in the US market for several stocks and indexes. As exotic options continue to gain popularity in the options trading world, it is expected that more and more exotic options will be standardized for trading in the public exchanges..

Here is a non-exhaustive list of well known exotic options:

Chooser Options
Exotic Options which determines if it is a call or put option only when a predetermined date is reached.

Look-back Options
The brainchild of Black-Scholes-Merton model co founder, Robert C. Merton. These are Exotic Options without a strike price. The holder of this kind of Exotic Options exercisesthe option at the best price achieved during the life of the option.

Shout Options
Exotic Options with 2 strike prices. One which was determined when the shout option was bought and another one determined at the discretion of the holder during the life of the shout option.

Asian Options
Exotic Options which pays off based on the average price of the underlying asset on a few specific dates.

Barrier Options
Exotic Options which comes into existence or goes out of existence when certain prices has been reached.

Binary Options
Exotic Options which pays you a fixed amount of money or the value of the underlying asset when the option expires in the money.

Power Options
Exotic Options which pays you an amount equal to the power of the value of the underlying asset above the strike price.

Basket Options
Exotic Options which is really a Plain-Vanilla option based on not one underlying asset but a group of underlying assets.

Exchange Options
Exotic Options giving the holder the right to exchange on kind of asset for another.

Extendible Options
Exotic Options which is a Plain-Vanilla option which allows the holder to extend the expiration date.

Compound Options
Exotic Options which is really an option which underlying asset is another option.

Range Options
Exotic Options which pays out based on the difference between the maximum and minimum price of the underlying asset during the life of the option.

Spread Options
Exotic Options which has the spread between 2 underlying assets as the underlying asset.

The most commonly used Exotic Options in option trading are the Look-Back Options and the Barrier Options.

Exotic Options - Difference Between Exotic Options & Standard Options

The table below summarizes the main differences between exotic options generally and plain vanilla options

exotic Options	Plain Vanilla Options
Customized	Standardized
OTC Traded	Publicly Traded
Many Types	Single Type
More Expensive	Cheaper
No Standard Pricing	Standardized Pricing Model

he pricing of exotic options, defined in most references as every option
type apart from the European and American vanilla options, is performed
either by using a closed formula or by relying on a numerical method to
evaluate the integral the pricing function involves. Whenever available, a
closed formula is more precise and requires less computational effort. This
is the reasoning behind our search for general closed formulas that unify
exotic option pricing.

The closed formulas for pricing exotic options have mainly been developed to price options whose payoffs exhibit one, and only one, very specific feature, and they assume an elementary market setup. However, the industry requirements go well beyond these simplifications. Exotic options underlying assets spread across several currency zones, and exotic options payoff profiles include features from multiple exotic option types.

This need to account for multiple features in a computationally simple process calls for a unification of the existing closed exotic option pricing formulas. Thus, instead of proceeding to develop formulas for specific option types, I propose a general approach that is able to accommodate several of the features seen in most exotics. Hence, I produce a formula for a generic payoff, covering thus all exotic options whose features are included in it. The market setting underlying the formula is also able to accommodate very diverse market setups, covering as many currency zones as needed.

Finally, the general formula allows the development of payoff languages. Payoff languages are extremely useful in industrial pricing applications as they enable the decoupling the payoff definition process from the pricing routines. Thus, as long as the payoff only uses the features covered by this general formula, the development of a new payoff profile does not necessitate the development of a new pricing routine. This means that industry agents can freely combine the desired features, while using the same pricing routines.

This paper is divided into four sections. This first section covers the mo-

tivation for the paper and the literature review. The second section develops
the model, the payoff of a generic claim and its pricing formula. Section
three then discusses the applications, including performance matters, and
provides examples and the final section concludes
Literature on exotic options is vast and dates back to the late 1970s. It
is not our intention to give a complete chronology of the works related to
this field but just to refer some landmark contributions for each of the main
threads of research. Compilations of exotic options descriptions and pricing
formulas may be found in Nelken (1995), Zhang (1997), Haug (1998), an Hakala and Wystup (2002).

According to my exotic option definition above, there are three threads
of research in exotics, the first of which deals with options on multiple under-
lyings. The distinctive characteristic of these options is their high sensitivity
to correlations. The landmark closed formulas were Margrabe (1978) - exchange options, Stulz (1982) maximum/minimum of two assets and Johnson
(1987) for several assets. One other thread deals with path-dependent options, namely lookback and barrier, which this paper only includes in their
discrete version. The main contributions on this thread are Rubinstein and
Reiner (1991) for barrier options and Goldman et al.(1979) and Conze and
Viswanathan (1991) for lookbacks. Further developments on barrier options were due to work by Heynen and Kat (1994), Carr (1995) and Wystup
(2003). For a remarkable description of the barrier option problem see Bj¨ork

(1998) whose general approach covers a wide class of payoffs. The last thread
deals with Asian option and basket options. Their distinctive characteristic
is the need to handle sums of geometric Brownian motions. Initial contributions for simpler geometric average problems are from Vorst (1992), and a
major development for arithmetic average problems is due to Ve˘ce˘r (2001).
The present paper extends previous work on this subject

2 Model Development

2.1 Model Description

The model on which I develop a closed formula can be classified as a
multivariate Black–Scholes model. It is a multi-asset model in which all
assets are tradable including for example stocks, currencies, precious metals
and indexes composed by these.

I assume the existence of n assets A_i, and the respective bank accounts
B_i where asset A_i may be deposited, with i $= 1, \ldots, n$. Each of the accounts
yields a return, in units of the same asset, at a continuosly compounded rate
of r_i. Such a rate may be interpreted as an interest rate of a currency or

1

as a repo rate of a stock. Although it is also common also to use this rate
to represent dividend payments for individual stocks, I advise against it
since dividend payments are typically not payed continuously and are not
proportional to the asset price, see [22] for details. Each bank account thus
follows the dynamics

$$dB_i(t)/B_i(t) = r_i(t)dt. \quad (1)$$

I furthermore assume the existence of one, and only one, price pro-

cess for each asset A_i allowing its expression in units of
another asset A_j .

This structure is usually referred to as a tree structure.
Though here the
definition of the root (asset) of the tree is not critical, any
asset can play
that role, what is critical is to have one path, and only one
path, to express
the price of one asset in terms of any other. Such a
structure excludes tri-
angular relationships as for example EUR/USD, USD/JPY
and EUR/JPY
foreign exchange pairs. I exclude these relationships
because they impose
restrictions on the volatilities and correlations between the
assets, see [10]
for details.
Hence, we assume the existence of price processes S_{ij} ,
that is the price
of one unit of A_i expressed in units of A_j , with the
dynamics following the
stochastic differential equation (SDE)
Although other setups are also plausible, we choose this
one for three
reasons: it is general enough to accommodate most exotic
options I have
encountered, the formulas generated are still manageable,
and the volatil-
ities and correlations can be freely specified. Figure 1
illustrates a model
setup that would underlie the valuation of a typical
structured product that
depends on several equity indexes spread across the
world

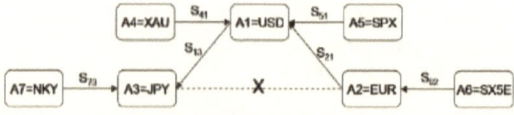

Figure 1: Example of market setup. The abbreviations
refer to the follow-

ing: USD to United States dollars, EUR to the euro currency, JPY to the
Japanese yen, XAU to the gold ounce, SPX to the S&P500 index, SX5E to
the DJ Eurostoxx 50 index, and NKY to the Nikkei index.
It shows a market with seven assets and six prices. It includes the
currencies of the three main monetary zones and the most popular indexes
of each. The currency pairs S_{21} and S_{13} are the most liquid and are defined
according to market standards, EUR/USD and USD/JPY respectively. The
prices of the baskets of stocks that compose each of the equity indexes A_5,

A_6 and A_7 are naturally expressed in terms of their respective currencies

A Bermudan Option is a type of nonstandard American option with early exercise restricted to certain dates during the life of the option. Bermudan Options have an "early exercise" date and expiration date. Before the "early exercise" date, it behaves like a European Option because it can not be exercised. After the "early exercise" date, the option behaves like an American Option because it can be exercised at any time up until expiration.

A Bermudan put option on a stock gives its holder the right to sell the stock at an agreed strike price at a certain finite number of fixed times before or at the final expiry time. Thus a Bermudan put option is more valuable than a European option (with the same parameters) but less valuable than an American put option, which can be exercised at any time before expiry. This Demonstration implements the famous method due to Longstaff and Schwartz of computing the price of a Bermudan put option on a stock by Monte Carlo simulation. Although the method can be applied to any model of stock movement, here I use it in the case of the classical Black–Scholes model. For simplicity, I also assume that the stock pays no dividend.

he Binomial options pricing model approach has been widely used since it is able to handle a variety of conditions for which other models cannot easily be applied. This is largely because the BOPM is based on the description of an underlying instrument over a period of time rather than a single point. As a consequence, it is used to value American options that are exercisable at any time in a given interval as well as Bermudan options that are exercisable at specific instances of time. Being relatively simple, the model is readily implementable in computer software (including a spreadsheet).

Although computationally slower than the Black–Scholes formula, it is more accurate, particularly for longer-dated options on securities with dividend payments. For these reasons, various versions of the binomial model are widely used by practitioners in the options markets.[citation needed]

For options with several sources of uncertainty (e.g., real options) and for options with complicated features (e.g., Asian options), binomial methods are less practical due to several difficulties, and Monte Carlo option models are commonly used instead. When simulating a small number of time steps Monte Carlo simulation will be more computationally time-consuming than BOPM (cf. Monte Carlo methods in finance). However, the worst-case runtime of BOPM will be $O(2^n)$, where n is the number of time steps in the simulation. Monte Carlo simulations will generally have a polynomial time complexity, and will be faster for large numbers of simulation steps. Monte Carlo simulations are also less susceptible to sampling errors, since binomial techniques use discrete time units. This becomes more true the smaller the discrete units become.

Step 1: Create the binomial price tree

The tree of prices is produced by working forward from valuation date to expiration.

At each step, it is assumed that the underlying instrument will move up or down by a specific factor

(or   ) per step of the tree (where, by definition,

      and   ). So, if   is the current price, then in

the next period the price will either be   or   .
The up and down factors are calculated using the

underlying volatility,   , and the time duration of a step,

      , measured in years (using the day count convention of the underlying instrument). From the

condition that the variance of the log of the price is   , I have:

Above is the original Cox, Ross, & Rubinstein (CRR) method; there are other techniques for generating the lattice, such as "the equal probabilities" tree. The Trinomial tree is a similar model, allowing for an up, down or stable path.

The CRR method ensures that the tree is recombinant, i.e. if the underlying asset moves up and then down (u,d), the price will be the same as if it had moved down and then up (d,u)—here the two paths merge or recombine. This property reduces the number of tree nodes, and thus accelerates the computation of the option price.

This property also allows that the value of the underlying asset at each node can be calculated directly via formula, and does not require that the tree be built first. The node-value will be:

Where   is the number of up ticks and   is the number of down ticks.

Swap

Derivatives contracts can be divided into two general families:

1. Contingent claims, e.g. options

2. Forward claims, which include exchange-traded futures, forward contracts, and swaps

A swap is an agreement between two parties to exchange sequences of cash flows for a set period of time. Usually, at the time the contract is initiated, at least one of these series of cash flows is determined by a random or uncertain variable, such as an interest rate, foreign exchange rate, equity price or commodity price. Conceptually, one may view a swap as either a portfolio of forward contracts or as a long position in one bond coupled with a short position in another bond. This article will discuss the two most common and most basic types of swaps: the plain vanilla interest rate and currency swaps.

The Swaps Market

Unlike most standardized options and futures contracts, swaps are not exchange-traded instruments. Instead, swaps are customized contracts that are traded in the over-the-counter (OTC) market between private parties. Firms and financial institutions dominate the swaps market, with few (if any) individuals ever participating. Because swaps occur on the OTC market, there is always the risk of a counterparty defaulting on the swap.

The first interest rate swap occurred between IBM and the World Bank in 1981. However, despite their relative youth, swaps have exploded in popularity. In 1987, the International Swaps and Derivatives Association reported that the swaps market had a total notional value of $865.6 billion. By mid-2006, this figure exceeded $250 trillion, according to the Bank for International Settlements. That's more than 15 times the size of the U.S. public equities market.

Plain Vanilla Interest Rate Swap

The most common and simplest swap is a "plain vanilla" interest rate swap. In this swap, Party A agrees to pay Party B a predetermined, fixed rate of interest on a notional principal on specific dates for a specified period of time. Concurrently, Party B agrees to make payments based on a floating interest rate to Party A on that same notional principal on the same specified dates for the same specified time period. In a plain vanilla swap, the two cash flows are paid in the same currency. The specified payment dates are called settlement dates, and the times between are called settlement periods. Because swaps are customized contracts, interest payments may be made annually, quarterly, monthly, or at any other interval determined by the parties.

For example, on Dec. 31, 2006, Company A and Company B enter into a five-year swap with the following terms:

- Company A pays Company B an amount equal to 6% per annum on a notional principal of $20 million.
- Company B pays Company A an amount equal to one-year LIBOR + 1% per annum on a notional principal of $20 million.

LIBOR, or London Interbank Offer Rate, is the interest rate offered by London banks on deposits made by other banks in the Eurodollar markets. The market for interest rate swaps frequently (but not always) uses LIBOR as the base for the floating rate. For simplicity, let's assume the two parties exchange payments annually on December 31, beginning in 2007 and concluding in 2011.

At the end of 2007, Company A will pay Company B $20,000,000 * 6% = $1,200,000. On Dec. 31, 2006, one-year LIBOR was 5.33%; therefore, Company B will pay Company A $20,000,000 * (5.33% + 1%) = $1,266,000. In a plain vanilla interest rate swap, the floating rate is usually determined at the beginning of the settlement period. Normally, swap contracts allow for payments to be netted against each other to avoid unnecessary payments. Here, Company B pays $66,000, and Company A pays nothing. At no point does the principal change hands, which is why it is referred to as a "notional" amount. Figure 1 shows the cash flows between the parties, which occur annually (in this example).

Plain Vanilla Foreign Currency Swap
The plain vanilla currency swap involves exchanging principal and fixed interest payments on a loan in one currency for principal and fixed interest payments on a similar loan in another currency. Unlike an interest rate swap, the parties to a currency swap will exchange principal amounts at the beginning and end of the swap. The two specified principal amounts are set so as to be approximately equal to one another, given the exchange rate at the time the swap is initiated.

For example, Company C, a U.S. firm, and Company D, a European firm, enter into a five-year currency swap for $50 million. Let's assume the exchange rate at the time is $1.25 per euro (e.g. the dollar is worth 0.80 euro). First, the firms will exchange principals. So, Company C pays $50 million, and Company D pays 40 million euros. This satisfies each company's need for funds denominated in another currency (which is the reason for the swap).

As with interest rate swaps, the parties will actually net the payments against each other at the then-prevailing exchange rate. If at the one-year mark, the exchange rate is $1.40 per euro, then Company C's payment equals $1,960,000, and Company D's payment would be $4,125,000. In practice, Company D would pay the net difference of $2,165,000 ($4,125,000 - $1,960,000) to Company C.Then, at intervals specified in the swap agreement, the parties will exchange interest payments on their respective principal amounts. To keep things simple, let's say they make these payments annually, beginning one year from the exchange of principal. Because Company C has borrowed euros, it must pay interest in euros based on a euro interest rate. Likewise, Company D, which borrowed dollars, will pay interest in dollars, based on a dollar interest rate. For this example, let's say the agreed-upon dollar-denominated interest rate is 8.25%, and the euro-denominated interest rate is 3.5%. Thus, each year, Company C pays 40,000,000 euros * 3.50% = 1,400,000 euros to Company D.

Company D will pay Company C $50,000,000 * 8.25% = $4,125,000.

Finally, at the end of the swap (usually also the date of the final interest payment), the parties re-exchange the original principal amounts. These principal payments are unaffected by exchange rates at the time. Who Would Use a Swap?

The motivations for using swap contracts fall into two basic categories: commercial needs and comparative advantage. The normal business operations of some firms lead to certain types of interest rate or currency exposures that swaps can alleviate. For example, consider a bank, which pays a floating rate of interest on deposits (e.g. liabilities) and earns a fixed rate of interest on loans (e.g. assets). This mismatch between assets and liabilities can cause tremendous difficulties. The bank could use a fixed-pay swap (pay a fixed rate and receive a floating rate) to convert its fixed-rate assets into floating-rate assets, which would match up well with its floating-rate liabilities.

Some companies have a comparative advantage in acquiring certain types of financing. However, this comparative advantage may not be for the type of financing desired. In this case, the company may acquire the financing for which it has a comparative advantage, then use a swap to convert it to the desired type of financing.

For example, consider a well-known U.S. firm that wants to expand its operations into Europe, where it is less known.

It will likely receive more favorable financing terms in the U.S. By using a currency swap, the firm ends up with the euros it needs to fund its expansion.

CMS SWAP

CMS swap is a kind of second order swap where you swap a rate of your choice against the above mentioned '10 year swap rate'. Every once in a while the rate is changed by referencing whatever Reuters says on that date the '10 year swap rate' is. Because it is always the 10 year rate that is referenced, it is called a constant maturity (in this case 10 year maturity) swap. Your payments however vary depending on developments in the market for ordinary swaps.

A constant maturity swap (CMS) rate for a given tenor is referenced as a point on the Swap curve. A swap curve itself is a term structure wherein every point on the curve is the effective par swap rate for that tenor. This is analogous to a 3m LIBOR curve represents 3m forward rates for a given tenor.

A swap rate can be considered as a weighted-average of forward rates. e.g. a two year par swap rate would be the fixed rate that makes a swap on (assume) LIBOR have NPV zero at inception. Usually, a LIBOR curve (or more generically a forward curve) would be bootstrapped using swap rates in the market (usually from 2y on-wards).

For almost all derivatives you mentioned (best of my knowledge) you can liken them to their LIBOR counterpart where the reference curve is the par swap curve (effective swap rates per tenor) in lieu of the 3m LIBOR curve. e.g. a

CMS swap's floating leg will (on fixing day) not refer the 3m LIBOR but the swap rate for the tenor instead.

Moreover, one could also have the other leg floating and refer to LIBOR underlying curve. E.g. a 6m LIBOR v/s 2Y CMS swap will have one leg will pay 6m LIBOR for any fixing date v/s the other leg which will pay par 2Y swap rate for the fixing date.

A Constant Maturity Swap (CMS) swap is a swap where one of the legs pays (respectively receives) a swap rate of a fixed maturity, while the other leg receives (respectively pays) fixed (most common) or floating. A CMT swap is very similar to a CMS swap, with the exception that one pays the par yield of a Treasury bond, note or bill instead of the swap rate. More generally, one calls Constant Maturity Swap and Constant Maturity Treasury derivatives, derivatives that refer to a swap rate of a given maturity or a pay yield of a bond, note or bill with a constant maturity. Since most likely, treasury issued on the market will not exactly match the maturity of the reference rate, one needs to interpolate market yield. (rates published by the British Banker Association in Europe and by the Federal Reserve Bank of New York) MARKETING OF THESE PRODUCTS CMT and CMS swaps provide a flexible and market efficient access to long dated interest rates. On the liability side, CMS and CMT swaps offer the ability to hedge long-dated positions. Great clients have been life insurers as they are heavily indebted in long dated payment obligations. Generous insurance policies need to be hedged against the sharp rise of the back end of the interest rate curve. Typical trade is a swap where they received the swap rate. On the asset side, corporate and other financial institutions have heavily invested in CMS market to enjoy yield enhancement and diversified funding. In a very steep curve environment, swaps paying CMS look very attractive to clients that think that the swap rates would not go as high as the market (and the forward curve) is pricing. Alternatively, in a flat yield curve environment, swaps receiving CMS look very attractive to market participants thinking that swap rates would rise in the futures as a consequence of the steepening of the curve. In a swap where one pays Libor plus a spread versus receiving CMS 10 year, the structure is mainly sensitive to the slope of the interest rate yield curve and is almost immunized against any parallel shift of the interest rate yield curve. For all these reasons, it is not surprising that the CMS markets and the CMS options markets now trade in large quantities, both interbank and between corporates and financial institutions. Pricing Because of the increasing size of the CMS market, the market has seen its margin eroding. Banks have developed more and more advanced models to account for the smile, resulting in first a more pronounced smile and also an increasingly spread between CMS swap and their swaption hedge. There exist two different methodologies for pricing CMS swaps: Parametric computation of the CMS convexity correction (See Hull(200), Benhamou (1999) and (2000)). In this approach, one assumes a model and uses some (smart) approximation methods to compute the expected swap rate under the forward measure. Non parametric computation of the swap rates. This approach assumes Non parametric computation of the CMS rates. This approach tries to minimize the amount of hypothesis between the computation of the CMS rate (see the works of Amblard, Lebuchoux (2000), Pugachevsky (2001)). Note also that practitioners focus heavily on the computation of the forward CMS as they use these modified forwards and the volatility read from swaption market to compute simple options on CMS (CMS cap and floor, CMS swaption). This practice is justified by the fact that the first order effect comes mainly from the convexity corrected forwards as opposed to modified volatility assumptions. Using the same vol is therefore right at first order approximation, and strictly right in a Black Scholes setting. Let use derive shortly the sketch lines of the two methods mentioned above. First, one can rapidly see that pricing a CMS swap boils down to price a simple swap rate received at time T. This can be done under the forward measure forward neutral measure QT , leading to

$$E^{Q_T}\left[Sw(T,T_1,...,T_n)\right],$$

compute:

where $E^{Q_T}\left[\ \right]$ is the expectation under the forward neutral measure Q_T,

and $Sw(T,T_1,...,T_n)$ the value at time T of the swap rate with fixed payment

dates $T_1,...,T_n$.

We can then use standard change of numeraire technique to change the expression above. The natural numeraire for the swap rate is the annuity (also called level or dvo1, defined as the pv of one basis points paid over the life of the forward Sthis leads to

wap rate) of the swap rate, denoted by

$$LVL(T).$$

$$E^{Q_T}\left[Sw(T,T_1,...,T_n)\right]=E^{LVL_T}\left[\frac{B(T,T)}{LVL(T)}*\frac{LVL(0)}{B(0,T)}*Sw(T,T_1,...,T_n)\right],$$

$$\text{since } \frac{dQ_T}{dQ^{LVL_T}}=\frac{B(T,T)}{LVL(T)}*\frac{LVL(0)}{B(0,T)}.$$

This shows that the CMS rate is equal to the swap rate plus an extra term function of the covariance under the annuity measure between the forward swap rate and the forward annuity:

$$E^{Q_T}\left[Sw(T,T_1,...,T_n)\right]$$

$$= Sw(0,T_1,...,T_n) + CovQ^{LVL_T}\left(\frac{LVL(0)B(T,T)}{LVL(T)B(0,T)}, Sw(T,T_1,...,T_n)\right)$$

As a result, the CMS rate depends on the following three components: The yield curve via the swap rate and the annuity. The volatility of the forward annuity and the forward swap rate.

 The correlation between the forward annuity and the forward swap rate.

Swaption

Swaptions: A better way to express a short duration view

Many pension plan sponsors have a view that interest rates will rise and express this view by having a duration of assets significantly shorter than the duration of liabilities. If interest rates do rise then many of these pension plan sponsors will likely happily add more long duration assets to the plan in order to reduce the duration mismatch between assets and liabilities. It is my view that for plan sponsors who are short duration today due to a view on rates but committed to hedging more if and when rates rise, swaptions can be used to more efficiently express this short duration "hedge later" mindset. First, we find that selling payer swaptions can be used to simply monetize interest rate triggers and/or sell away funded status upside that has little value. If a plan sponsor has conviction that they will add duration when a target level of rates is achieved, selling a payer swaption allows them to collect a premium by committing to do so (if rates do rise beyond the target level) today. If rates do not rise to the target level, then the premium is realized and the plan's funded status is improved (relative to remaining unhedged) and if rates do rise beyond the target level, then the plan sponsor is forced to lengthen the duration of assets which is likely what they would do anyway. Second, we find that plan sponsors can take the premium received by selling payer swaptions to purchase valuable downside protection by buying a lower strike receiver swaption. This is typically done on a zero up-front cost basis by matching the premium of the receiver swaption with that of the payer swaption. We conclude that these so called zero-cost swaption collars are particularly well aligned with the pension risk management objectives of plan sponsors. A plan sponsor can sell away upside that is either of little benefit or associated with rate levels where the plan sponsor will likely hedge regardless in exchange for more highly valued downside protection in case rates actually fall. We believe this is a more efficient way to express a short duration mindset within a pension risk management context. Last, we assess the current pricing of swaptions. We find that swaptions are attractively priced as you can sell away upside today for a significantly higher price than what is needed to purchase a symmetrical amount of downside protection - meaning that it appears to be a favorable time to be executing such swaption strategies.

For pension plan sponsors adopting a Liability Driven Investing (LDI) strategy, the combination of low interest rates and low funding ratios continues to impede the amount of interest rate risk plan sponsors decide to hedge within their pension plans. Strategically, most LDI adopters acknowledge the benefits of hedging a large proportion of their interest rate risk (my views on the appropriate amount were discussed in white paper - "Level 2 LDI: Three key implementation considerations"). As a result, most sponsors have at least extended the duration of the fixed income portfolio in order to hedge a portion of the plan's interest rate risk. However, they choose to be tactically short duration (typically by a wide margin) relative to their optimal strategic interest rate hedge ratio in light of the current low interest rate and funding ratio environment. This amounts to a (typically very large) bet that interest rates will rise causing an improvement in funded status as the present value of liabilities decreases in value more than the assets do. While we can certainly understand today's desire to be short of the strategic interest rate hedge ratio, we encourage our clients to consider (and have seen both US and UK LDI clients increasingly implement) option-based strategies to express this view on interest rates in a more risk controlled manner. Our view is that swaptions, and in particular zerocost swaption collars, are a more efficient means for pension plans to express this interest rate view as opposed to being outright short duration versus the long-term strategic level of interest rate hedging. As will be discussed in more detail later, this is particularly true based on the current market pricing of these types of swaption strategies.

Before we discuss the mechanics of swaptions and potential applications to managing interest rate risk, we need to clarify how we are defining interest rate risk. The biggest year-toyear liability risk plan sponsors face is the pension discount rate falling, causing an increase in the present value of the pension liabilities. Importantly, pension discount rate risk can be caused by two different market scenarios (1) Treasury rates falling and/or (2) A-AAA credit spreads narrowing. We refer to the former as interest rate risk and the latter as credit spread risk. Each of these risks needs to be explicitly managed and our focus in this paper is how swaptions can be used to manage the interest rate risk component as opposed to the credit spread risk component of overall discount rate risk. Conceptually, a swaption can be thought of as an option on the value of a bond. Given that the value of liabilities behave similarly to the value of long duration bonds, swaptions can be thought of as an option on the value of pension liabilities. Within this liability risk management context, swaptions can be purchased to provide some protection against increases in the value of the liabilities if interest rates were to fall and/or swaptions can be sold to forgo some of the upside attributable to the value of liabilities falling if interest rates were to rise. Taking this one step further, when working with pension clients to manage funding ratio outcomes, we typically see swaptions being used in two ways (often in combination with one another). First, to provide protection against funded status drawdowns by increasing interest rate hedging (gaining exposure to liability matching bonds) if interest rates fall below a certain level - this can be achieved by buying a

low strike receiver swaption. Second, sell away funded status upside attributable to rising interest rates beyond a certain level and/or lock in interest rates at more attractive levels - this can be done by selling a high strike payer swaption. Below we provide an example for each in turn. Buy Receiver Swaption – buying protection against falling rates Technically speaking, the buyer of a receiver swaption has the right, but not the obligation to enter into a receive fixed, pay floating (LIBOR) par swap of a specified maturity (e.g. 30 year par swap) on a specified date in the future at a specified fixed rate1 . Buying a low strike receiver swaption is analogous to buying protection against falling interest rates and the resultant increase in the value of liabilities.

As with all strategies which meet the objectives of a plan sponsor, it is extremely important to overlay whether the strategy is sensible in light of current market conditions. In fact, we have found that for our clients the pricing of the swaption market at time of implementation has had significant influence over each point of customization discussed above. Further, as pricing changes over the life of the swaption it has a significant influence over when and how it is most appropriate to restructure the strategy.

Swaptions, like any other LDI-oriented implementation are not set-it and forget-it strategies. As a means to help explain why pricing is now influential in the management of these strategies, we start by explaining what we mean by the pricing of the swaption market. The main market factors which drive the pricing (premium paid or received) of swaptions are: • Moneyness: This is the difference between the strike rate and the current ATMF rate. The ATMF rate is the market's current expectation of where the swap rate underlying the swaption will be at the maturity date. The closer the ATMF rate is to either rising above (in the case of a high strike payer swaption) or falling below (in the case of a low strike receiver swaption) the strike, the higher the premium, and • Volatility: This is the expected volatility of interest rates. The higher the expected volatility the higher the premium as large increases in intrinsic value are more likely to occur. Importantly, the expected volatility varies by the strike rate, underlying swap maturity, and option maturity. Therefore, the relative attractiveness of swaption pricing can also vary by these key parameters as well. In our experience, plan sponsors tend to focus on the pricing of zero-cost collars. This can be done tracking the difference in pricing between a sold high strike payer swaption and a bought low strike receiver swaption. An ideal market environment is one where high strike swaptions are priced high (as these are being sold, this maximizes the premium received) and low strike swaptions are priced cheaply (as these are being purchased). This is because pension plans are typically either trying to sell a high strike payer swaption on a standalone basis or combining that with a premium equivalent low strike receiver. The most common way to track the relative pricing between high strike and low strike swaptions is to track what is called the volatility skew. Volatility skew is simply the difference in implied volatility between options on high rates and options on low rates. Figure 7 illustrates volatility skew for 2 year swaptions on 5, 10 and 30 year rates, which is a simple measure of the difference in volatility between the payer and the receiver. Our measure of normalized skew measures the difference in implied volatility of a payer swaption struck at the ATMF rate + 1%, and a receiver swaption struck at the ATMF rate − 1%. For plan sponsors choosing to be tactically short interest rate duration in the anticipation of higher levels of interest rates in the future, we find that swaptions can be an efficient tool in the LDI toolbox. Swaptions can be used to better manage funding ratio outcomes by either monetizing interest rate triggers (by selling payer swaptions) or to more attractively express a short duration view (by implementing a zero-cost swaption collar). In particular, zero-cost swaption collars are a good fit with the pension risk management objectives of plan sponsors. A plan sponsor can sell away upside that is either of little benefit or associated with rate levels where the plan sponsor will likely hedge anyway in exchange for more highly valued downside protection in case rates actually fall. We believe this is a more efficient way to express a short duration mindset within a pension risk management context. Further, zero-cost swaption collars look attractively priced in a historic context, meaning that it seems a favorable time to be executing such a strategy.

Rates quants need no introduction to the stochastic alpha, beta, rho (SABR) model.

Widely used to price European swaptions, the model has a useful expansion that allows users to calibrate it to the market-implied volatility surface analytically. The ease with which this can be done has made the model very popular, despite the fact it produces prices that can be arbitraged.

The implied volatility expansion – commonly called the Hagan expansion – doesn't really capture the dynamics of the swaptions at the high and low strikes, especially for longer maturities, making mispricing increasingly likely.

One way to obtain arbitrage-free prices is by using numerical techniques to calibrate the SABRmodel by solving a partial differential equation (PDE).

R
Implementation
CONSTANT

```r
EPS <- 10^(-8)


# sub function for SABR BS-IV

.x <- function(z, r){log((sqrt(1-2*r*z+z^2)+z-r)/(1-r))}

.z <- function(f, K, a, b, nu){nu/a*(f*K)^(0.5*(1-b))*log(f/K)}


# variable transformation function

.t1  <- function(x){1/(1+exp(x))}

.t2  <- function(x){2/(1+exp(x)) -1}


# Black-Scholes IV apporoximation formula by Hagan(2002)

SABR.BSIV <- function(t, f, K, a, b, r, n)

{

  z <- .z(f, K, a, b, n)

  x <- .x(z, r)

  numerator  <- 1 + ((1-b)^2/24*a^2/(f*K)^(1-b) +
```

```r
  0.25*r*b*n*a/(f*K)^(0.5*(1-b)) + (2-
3*r^2)*n^2/24)*t

  denominator <- x*(f*K)^(0.5*(1-b))*(1 +
(1-b)^2/24*(log(f/K))^2 + (1-
b)^4/1920*(log(f/K))^4)

  ifelse(abs((f-K)/f) < EPS,
a*numerator/f^(1-b),
z*a*numerator/denominator)

}


# Parameter calibration function for
SABR

SABR.calibration <- function(t, f, K, iv)

{

  # objective function for optimization

  # variables are transformed because of
satisfing the constraint conditions

  objective <- function(x){sum( (iv -
SABR.BSIV(t, f, K, exp(x[1]), .t1(x[2]),
.t2(x[3]), exp(x[4])))^2) }

  x <- nlm(objective, c(0.1, 0.5, 0.0, 0.1))

  # return the optimized parameters

  parameter <- x$estimate

  parameter <- c(exp(parameter[1]),
.t1(parameter[2]), .t2(parameter[3]),
exp(parameter[4]))

  names(parameter) <- c("Alpha", "Beta",
```

"Rho", "Nu")

parameter

}

The swaptions market is not new to pricing issues. When European rates plunged into negative territory in 2012, the SABR models used to price swaptions **started producing nonsensical values** – a phenomenon that was observed even at low positive rates. This triggered many valuation disputes and pushed quants to come up with techniques to solve the negative rates problem.

More recently, the industry decided to shift to a new pricing methodology to bring European cash-settled swaption prices in line with the underlying swaps – a mismatch that had been ignored for years until the difference **started to get magnified** by falling rates.

While the breakdown of models under negative rates is a more recent problem, the issue of arbitrageable prices has always existed.

To fix this, most firms typically apply some kind of crude adjustment to their existing implementation of the SABR model, which reduces the arbitrage instead of eliminating it completely.

"Most places use some kind of SABR variant usually with proprietary adjustments to mitigate the arbitrage, and there are quite a variety of approaches there. For example, some people might patch on a different low wing tail from a different distribution," says Roos. "Other people just try to make ad hoc adjustments to the implied volatility formula itself. Quite a few of these methods mitigate the arbitrage rather than removing it completely and people typically just live with whatever is left over."

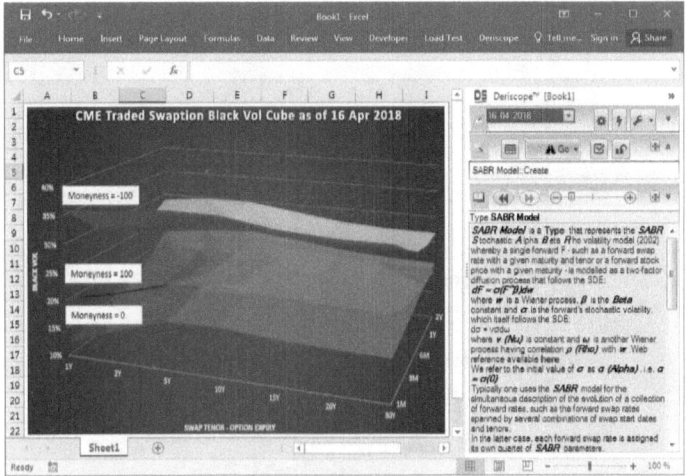

The pricing of exotic *interest rate* products cannot ignore the so called *market volatility cube* that is made daily available by several *swaption* brokers.

Traders often use the *SABR Stochastic volatility* model in order to estimate vols off the provided grid.

how to price an out-of-the-money *swaption* by applying *SABR*calibration on the *volatility cube*

CME clears *European swaption* trades
with **5** different *expiries* - **1M, 3M, 6M, 1Y, 2Y** –
and **7**underlying swap tenors - **1Y, 2Y, 5Y, 10Y, 15Y, 20Y, 30Y**.

Below you see the *at-the-money Black vols* quoted as of **16 Apr 2018**

LogNormal Vols for strike offset 0							
0	1Y	2Y	5Y	10Y	15Y	20Y	30Y
1M	12,4559%	15,6906%	18,5884%	18,7795%	18,0630%	17,7101%	17,5578%
3M	14,1064%	17,1848%	19,5244%	19,6338%	18,9183%	18,5667%	18,4021%
6M	15,3294%	18,1170%	20,7427%	20,7399%	19,9287%	19,5322%	19,3833%
1Y	17,7833%	20,1802%	22,1637%	21,9932%	21,0658%	20,5908%	20,3785%
2Y	22,1572%	23,2539%	23,9005%	23,0334%	21,9114%	21,2860%	21,0047%

The next image contains the *out-of-the-money Black vols* for the following *strike offsets* (in *basis points*) from the respective *atm strike*: ±200, ±100, ±50, ±25. Note that a few *strike-expiry-tenor*combinations are so illiquid that no data are available.

LogNormal Vols for strike offset -25							
-25	1Y	2Y	5Y	10Y	15Y	20Y	30Y
1M	16.1224%	18.7759%	21.1707%	21.2160%	20.4002%	20.0122%	19.8596%
3M	16.9077%	19.5302%	21.4918%	21.4442%	20.6626%	20.2812%	20.1363%
6M	17.2840%	19.7721%	#N/A	#N/A	#N/A	#N/A	#N/A
1Y	19.1239%	21.4288%	#N/A	#N/A	#N/A	#N/A	#N/A
2Y	23.3314%	24.4099%	#N/A	#N/A	#N/A	#N/A	#N/A

LogNormal Vols for strike offset 25							
25	1Y	2Y	5Y	10Y	15Y	20Y	30Y
1M	12.1184%	15.1927%	18.5501%	19.1003%	18.4223%	18.0859%	17.9512%
3M	13.1751%	16.2615%	19.1336%	19.5366%	18.8505%	18.5098%	18.3513%
6M	14.2440%	17.3007%	#N/A	#N/A	#N/A	#N/A	#N/A
1Y	16.8889%	19.1389%	#N/A	#N/A	#N/A	#N/A	#N/A
2Y	21.2621%	22.5582%	#N/A	#N/A	#N/A	#N/A	#N/A

LogNormal Vols for strike offset -50							
-50	1Y	2Y	5Y	10Y	15Y	20Y	30Y
1M	21.5083%	23.4519%	25.5179%	25.6013%	24.6235%	24.1796%	24.0454%
3M	20.7284%	22.9278%	24.7304%	24.6510%	23.7625%	23.3528%	23.2295%
6M	19.3622%	22.1456%	24.2394%	23.9487%	23.0723%	22.6602%	22.5841%
1Y	20.9093%	23.0879%	24.6450%	24.2814%	23.3367%	22.8955%	22.7349%
2Y	24.8170%	25.8622%	26.1768%	25.1529%	24.0049%	23.3974%	23.2039%

LogNormal Vols for strike offset 50							
50	1Y	2Y	5Y	10Y	15Y	20Y	30Y
1M	14.8978%	17.2127%	20.2511%	21.0660%	20.3587%	20.0071%	19.8616%
3M	14.0414%	16.9106%	19.9357%	20.5495%	19.8882%	19.5514%	19.4050%
6M	14.2861%	17.2236%	20.1530%	20.7470%	19.9838%	19.6021%	19.4512%
1Y	16.4050%	18.8483%	21.2240%	21.2809%	20.1766%	19.9112%	19.6697%
2Y	20.6162%	21.6925%	22.6565%	21.9672%	20.8778%	20.2487%	19.3330%

LogNormal Vols for strike offset -100							
-100	1Y	2Y	5Y	10Y	15Y	20Y	30Y
1M	36.1115%	36.4761%	37.5157%	37.4117%	36.0021%	35.4300%	35.4006%
3M	30.5621%	31.6620%	33.6734%	33.6621%	33.4824%	31.8810%	31.8150%
6M	27.0083%	28.6728%	30.6221%	30.1681%	29.1172%	28.8659%	28.6915%
1Y	25.7271%	27.7032%	28.9725%	28.4795%	27.4723%	27.0426%	27.0514%
2Y	28.8589%	29.8057%	29.8408%	28.6508%	27.4550%	26.8713%	28.8091%

LogNormal Vols for strike offset 100							
100	1Y	2Y	5Y	10Y	15Y	20Y	30Y
1M	20.7479%	22.6577%	25.0919%	25.9198%	25.0888%	24.8938%	24.5417%
3M	17.5946%	19.3349%	22.6442%	23.5797%	22.9614%	22.5117%	22.1693%
6M	15.6483%	18.3080%	21.5843%	23.2371%	21.4958%	21.1277%	20.9907%
1Y	16.3277%	18.6540%	21.2598%	21.5007%	20.6410%	20.1942%	19.9665%
2Y	19.9026%	20.9011%	22.1593%	21.5927%	20.5538%	19.9336%	19.6112%

LogNormal Vols for strike offset -200							
-200	1Y	2Y	5Y	10Y	15Y	20Y	30Y
1M	87.7743%	80.7015%	76.8300%	74.8240%	#N/A	#N/A	#N/A
3M	66.2899%	62.7704%	63.8677%	61.6416%	60.6912%	59.5767%	59.8672%
6M	51.8101%	51.5045%	53.4869%	52.3187%	50.2726%	49.5548%	50.0661%
1Y	42.9437%	44.3567%	45.7249%	44.8265%	43.2665%	42.7814%	43.3413%
2Y	43.9302%	44.7234%	44.3232%	42.4099%	40.7945%	40.2180%	40.7281%

LogNormal Vols for strike offset 200							
200	1Y	2Y	5Y	10Y	15Y	20Y	30Y
1M	#N/A	31.3429%	33.0882%	34.1884%	33.2720%	32.8571%	32.8391%
3M	23.6483%	25.7257%	27.9547%	29.0971%	28.2884%	27.8940%	27.7446%
6M	19.3030%	21.3316%	24.7629%	25.6218%	24.0338%	24.5240%	24.4022%
1Y	17.5553%	19.6098%	22.3782%	22.8442%	22.0528%	21.6434%	21.4498%
2Y	19.8162%	20.8097%	22.1196%	21.8365%	20.8897%	20.1047%	19.9991%

For any given set of parameters α, β, ν, ρ applying on a pair (T1,T2), the diffusion of the respective forward rate F(T1,T2) is known and therefore one is able to calculate the price of every European option that relies on that particular forward rate F(T1,T2).

This means, the prices of all European options differing on their strike K but sharing the same expiry T1 and underlying tenor T2 – T1 can be calculated.

In practice one considers only the pairs (T1,T2) that correspond to the European swaptions actually traded in the market, collects the available strikes K and finally

calculates the SABR-implied theoretical prices
SABR(T1,T2,K).

In practice again, one works with a reparametrization of
T1, T2, K in terms of т1, т2, k, where k is defined as the
spread K – ATM, where ATM is the at-the-money strike,
i.e. the known value of F(T1,T2) at time 0.

The reason for this reparametrization is twofold.

First, whereas T2 takes several different values as the
maturity dates of the various underlying swaps are mostly
different from each other, т2 takes only a few values since
several swaptions share the same tenor.

Second, no two swaptions share the same strike K, but
several share the same strike spread k.

The conclusion is that plotting the points (т1,т2,k) is far
easier than plotting the points (T1,T2,K), involves fewer
coordinates and results in a symmetrical 3-dimensional
lattice.

In the following image I deploy a 3-D coordinate system,
where the x axis represents the expiry interval т1, the y
axis the swap tenor т2 and the vertical z axis the strike
spread k. I consider three different values of k measured in
basis points, namely -100, 0 and 100 and use the same
combinations of т1, т2 as in the example above.

The result is nine points that represent **9** different
swaptions, arranged as three triplets, where each triplet
lies on the same vertical line corresponding to a fixed pair
(т1,т2).

Each triplet is then priced using the corresponding SABR
parameters that I had chosen in my earlier example and
the thus calculated price SABR(т1,т2,k) - quoted in terms
of the equivalent Black vol or normal vol - is displayed on
the side of each point.

The resulting grid along with the calculated prices is known
as the SABR-implied volatility cube

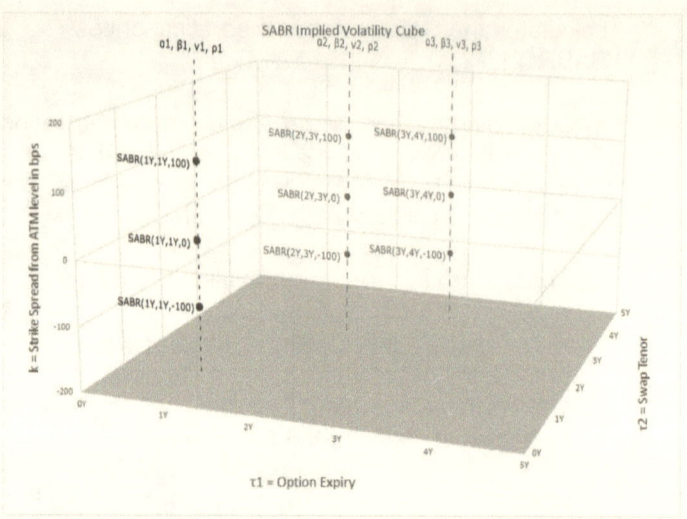

The market volatility cube is constructed by plotting the points (τ1,τ2,k) and then assigning to each point the actual market price Market(τ1,τ2,k) of the corresponding European swaption, quoted in terms of the equivalent Black or normal vol.

Continuing with the three swaptions example, the resulting diagram looks like that:

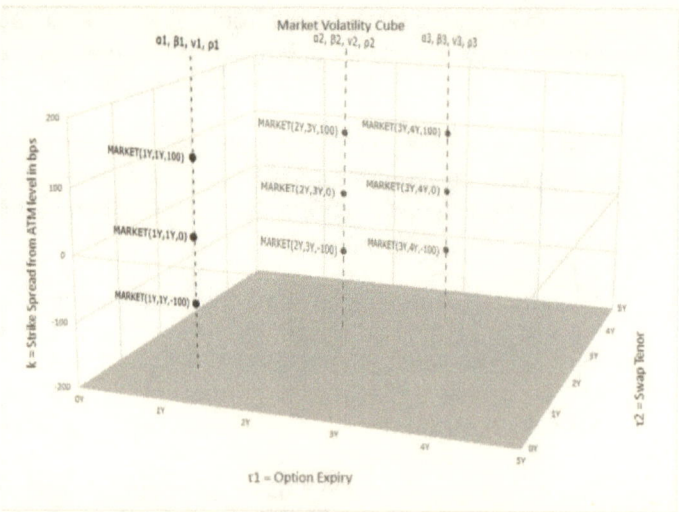

If I am interested in pricing a single European swaption for which the triplet (K,T1,T2) already corresponds to one of the grid points, then I should obviously use the appropriate vol read off the market volatility cube.

But if I need to price a European swaption for which the triplet (K,T1,T2) corresponds to a point (τ1,τ2,k) that falls between the grid points, then I am better off interpolating the α, β, v, ρ parameters of the neighboring points in the SABR cube and then extracting the corresponding vol than interpolating directly the vols of the neighboring points in the market volatility cube.

In practice, I achieve that by creating a Vol Curve object using a market volatility cube input as described above and feed that object to the pricing formula as part of the Market input.

I should also follow this approach when I price interest rate products the values of which depend on several forward rates, such as Bermudan swaptions and constant maturity swaps

Regulatory changes

In her keynote address, Valeria Sannucci, deputy governor of the Banca I will look at two building blocks: regulatory reform and transaction banking. We will begin with an overview and analysis of the plethora of banking regulation that is focused on the bank as a whole. Usually known by the term 'prudential regulation', the regulation of deposit-taking institutions aims to ensure the safety of customer deposits and stability of the financial system. This overview will constitute the background to understanding and analysing the potential impact and implications of all these changes to the business of global transaction banking. The overview will be followed by an in-depth explanation of what transaction banking services actually are – payments, trade finance and securities services – and how these services support the real economy at a local, regional and global level. Armed with these insights we can then analyse the effect of key regulatory reforms, such as Basel III, in the following chapters. Given the many uncertainties in the implementation of new banking regulation, this analysis cannot cover every consequence for transaction banking. However, it provides an essential overview of the key regulatory pillars that support banking services today and how these are impacted by twenty-first century law reform. Alongside the many intended consequences, there is also a risk of unintended consequences that some of these reforms could bring for the transaction banking business and thus the functioning of financial markets as well as the and growth of the global economy overall.

Even though international coordination of regulatory reforms has substantially increased – and we will review the new global regulatory architecture below – the array of regulatory developments is slowly but surely creating barriers to international finance, in the absence of a full analysis of their potential impacts on a deeply globalised, interconnected and digital world where business and financial flows are expected to be ubiquitous and far reaching. The regulatory floodgates have been opened far and wide but no one really knows at this stage what this will mean. In the old days, banking followed the simple pattern of, as the English put it, 'Borrow for £3, lend for £4 and go to the pub at 5 o'clock!' As it turns out, history has changed the course of this traditional banking business. Classical bank lending no longer generated sufficient revenue for banks and this is not a recent phenomenon. In consequence, some banks began to look into other ways to make money and in several cases this involved taking more risks. But it is clear that a number of factors played a role in pushing the overall systems into crisis. So let us now review some of the current regulatory proposals and high-level decisions that have thus far been put forward and partially implemented in reaction to the financial crisis; a crisis that is also often understood to be a US–European crisis, rather than a truly global one. After all, Latin American and Asian markets already went through their own crises during the 1990s and early 2000s, although even today the stability of some emerging market countries is certainly not a given. To my mind, some of the regulatory changes will have the power to completely change the face of banking ... and regulators, supervisors and politicians will need to consider the consequences and factor them into their future policy approach. For me the key question really is whether there is a future for global banking in any shape or form once the current list of regulatory measures – which continues to evolve – is implemented. In that regard, this book will also constitute a reminder of the benefits that a global universal highly diversified banking structure brings to the economy and how a mix of bank models ranging from small, medium and large with de-centralised or centralised set-ups actually supports the overall resilience of the global financial market. 2.1 What is in store for the global banking industry The first set of measures proposed in response to the financial crisis was a revision of the international framework for prudential supervision, or what we call for short 'Basel III'. The key amendments to the existing framework were focused on improving the quality and quantity of bank capital as well as introducing liquidity requirements and a cap on banks' leverage.

I will suggest here, however, that the regulation known as the Leverage Ratio has caused a distortionary reduction in the incentives of banks to intermediate markets for safe assets, especially the government securities repo market, without apparent financial stability benefits. I explain this with a simple model based on the notion of "debt overhang" introduced by Myers (1977). I will suggest adjustments to the leverage-ratio rule that would improve the liquidity of government securities markets and other low-risk high-importance markets, without sacrificing financial stability. I will describe how the other three core elements of financial-stability reform, those involving "too big to fail," derivatives markets, and shadow banking, are still well short of their goals in key areas. I will argue that the proposed single-point-of-entry method for the failure resolution of systemic financial firms is not yet ready for safe and successful deployment. A key success here, though, is that creditors of banks do appear to have gotten the message that in the future, their claims are much less likely to be bailed out. Derivatives reforms have forced huge amounts of swaps into central counterparties (CCPs), a major success in terms of collateralization and transparency in the swap market. As a result, however, CCPs are now themselves too big to fail. Effective operating plans and procedures for the failure resolution of CCPs have yet to be proposed. While the failure of a large CCP seems a remote possibility, this remoteness is difficult to verify because there is also no generally accepted regulatory framework for conducting CCP stress tests. This represents an undue lack of transparency. Reform of derivatives markets financial-stability regulation has mostly bypassed the market for foreign-exchange derivatives involving the delivery of one currency for another, a huge and systemically important class. Data repositories for the swaps market have not come close to meeting their intended purposes. Here especially, the opportunities of time afforded by the impetus of a severe crisis have not been used well. The biggest achievement in the area of shadow banking is the new set of rules governing money market mutual funds. Money funds of the constantnet-asset-value (CNAV) type can usually be redeemed at a constant value, despite fluctuations over time in the actual market value of their assets

Many investors therefore treat CNAV funds like bank deposits, and thus subject to a run whenever the redemption value of the funds could fall. This is exactly what happened on a massive scale in the United States when Lehman Brothers failed. In the U.S., after fits and starts that tested the influence of the Financial Stability Oversight Council, the Securities and Exchange Commission (SEC) has effectively forced CNAV money funds to invest only in government assets. Europe's regulatory reform of its money market funds has been delayed, but seems likely to follow the outlines of the US reforms. The G20 financial reforms have a wide range of other financial-stability objectives listed by the Financial Stability Board (2015b).5 For reasons of brevity and focus, however, I will not take the opportunity to address financial-stability regulatory reforms in these other areas. In addition to financial-stability regulation, legislatures decided that the time is ripe for improving the competitiveness and fairness of financial markets, and have asked regulators to enforce new price-transparency and tradecompetition requirements. To the extent that financial-stability regulations have reduced the incentives of bank-affiliated dealers to make markets, regulations in support of competitive transparent all-to-all trading can mitigate losses in market liquidity. Some markets can become even more liquid once dealer intermediation of over-the-counter markets is supplanted with all-to-all anonymous trading venues, and once there is less fragmentation of trade across off-exchange multilateral platforms. Some of the fragmentation is due to lack of international regulatory coordination. I will suggest that there is plenty of room for more progress in this area. The U.S. Dodd-Frank competition rules are narrowly aimed at the swap market. Europe's Markets in Financial

Instruments Directive (MiFID II) and proposed MIFIR implementing regulations are more ambitious in scope than

US reforms, but are moving much more slowly. Implementation of the most important trade-competition rules has been pushed back to early 2018. The costs of implementing and complying with regulation are among the tradeoffs for achieving greater financial stability. For example, in 2013 (even before the full regime of new regulations was in place) the six largest U.S. banks spent an estimated6 $70.2 billion on regulatory compliance, doubling the $34.7 billion they spent in 2007. Compliance requirements can accelerate or, potentially, decelerate overdue improvements in practices. 7 The frictional cost of complying with post-crisis regulations is easily exceeded by the total social benefits, but is nevertheless a factor to be considered when designing specific requirements and supervisory regimes. Delays in completing and implementing regulations (particularly in Europe) have been harmful, especially in light of the costs to businesses of regulatory uncertainty. Examples include delays in clarifying the implementation of MiFID II, as mentioned, and the 2012 Liikanen framework for ring-fencing and proprietary-trading limits for banks. This is not, however, the time to call a general halt to reforms in order to mitigate further costs and uncertainty. Continuing to put the significant remaining pieces of the reform into place, expeditiously, will add importantly to financial stability and market efficiency. Among the important contributors to post-crisis regulatory reform are the supra-national forums for regulatory standards setting, coordination, and peer review. Much has been accomplished, in particular, by the Financial Stability Board, the Basel Committee on Banking Supervsion, the Committee on Payments and Market Infrastructure (CPMI), and the International Organization of Securities Commissions (IOSCO). It is hard to imagine that progress would have been nearly as far reaching as it has been without the coordination of standards and the peer comparisons afforded by these groups. Overall, the international financial regulatory reform movement has made large strides and still has a lot to accomplish. Progress has not been easy because of the sheer complexity of the financial system, competing private interests, and differing national objectives.

Making Financial Institutions More Resilient I begin with a discussion of progress with the first of the core reform elements, "making financial institutions more resilient." Capital and Liquidity Regulations Thanks to the Basel III accords, the capital and liquidity cushions of the largest financial institutions are significantly higher than their pre-crisis levels. For example, the average Common Equity Tier 1 (CET1) capital ratios of the six largest U.S. bank holding companies (BHCs) has increased from typical pre-crisis levels of 7% to 7.5% of risk-weighted assets to over 12% during 2015.8 While CET1 ratios are measured on a somewhat different basis in the EU than in the US, the European Banking Authority (2015a) reports9 that the 15 largest EU banks had improved their CET1 ratios from about 9.6% at the end of 2009 to about 12.3% by the end of the second quarter of 2015. Over the same span of time, as shown in Figure 1, the fraction of all EU banks with CET1 ratios below 9% dropped from 36% to zero.10 This is a major achievement, and further improvements are planned. Adoption and implementation of the Basel III accords continues to make progress across the 27 member jurisdictions, as tracked by the Basel Commission on Banking Supervision (2016).

In addition to conventional requirements governing capital relative to riskweighted assets, Basel III includes a minimum "leverage ratio," of capital to total (not risk-weighted) assets. Beyond increasing capital requirements, the balance-sheet liquidity of large banks is now regulated to meet a minimum Liquidity Coverage Ratio (LCR), designed to ensure that cash outflows that could plausibly occur within 30 days are fully covered by ready cash sources. The LCR could be counterproductive, however, if it is not relaxed in times of stress so as to allow banks to actually access the liquidity sources that LCR requires. To my knowledge, this concern has not yet been addressed. A companion Basel-III liquidity regulation, the Net Stable Funding Ratio11 (NSFR), designed to limit maturity transformation, remains to be implemented. Kashyap, Tsomocos, and Vardoulakis (2014) explain the beneficial effect of multiple capital and liquidity requirements, given the multiple modalities for bank failure. Going further, the Fundamental Review of the Trading Book conducted by the Basel Commission on Banking Supervision has now completely revamped the measurement of market risk and risk weights for market risk. The Basel Committee on Banking Supervision (2016) summarizes progress here as follows. *"The deficiencies in the pre-crisis framework included an inadequate definition of the regulatory boundary between the banking book and trading book, which proved to be a key source of weakness in the design of the trading book regime. In addition, risk measurement methodologies were insufficiently robust. In particular, the models based capital framework for market risk relied (and still relies) heavily on risk drivers determined by banks, which has not always led to sufficient capital for the banking system as a whole. .... Compared to the current framework, the revised market risk capital standard is likely to result in an approximate median (weighted average) increase of 22% (40%) in total market risk capital "*

As a gauge of whether bank failures are as great a threat to market participants as they were before the implementation of resiliency reforms, Figure 2 shows the fraction of CDS referencing banks, versus non-banks, among the 15 most referenced corporations in the CDS market. Since early 2012, this fraction has declined from about 50% to about 28%. Currently, only Deutsche Bank and Barclays are in the top 15.

Banks are now less referenced by CDS, relative to non-banks

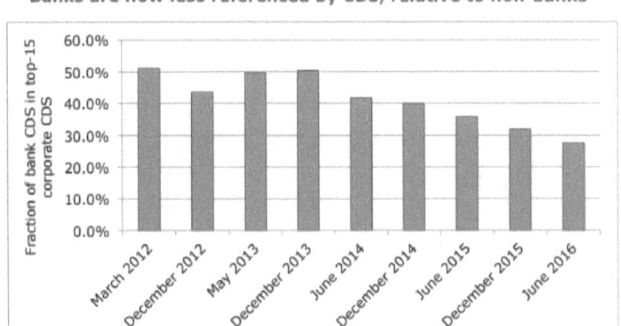

Unintended Consequences of Leverage Regulations There have nevertheless been some unintended adverse consequences of the new capital regulations. Most obvious among these, the "leverage ratio" requirement has impaired liquidity in the market for repurchase agreements backed by government securities, especially in the United States. As explained by the Financial Policy Committee of the Bank of England (2014c), the leverage-ratio rule is meant as a backstop for the risk-weightedasset capital requirement, because regulatory risk measures may not vary sufficiently with the true riskiness of assets. This can be a consequence of "regulatory arbitrage," as explained by Colliard (2014), Kiema and Jokivuolle (2014), and Begley, Purnanandam, and Zheng (2016). For example, in a sample of credit assets analyzed by the Basel Commission on Banking Supervsion (2013b), the capital levels assigned by the most conservative banks were about 50% higher than those for the least conservative banks. The leverage-ratio rule simply avoids the issue of risk measurement by assigning the same amount of required capital per unit of gross assets, regardless of the type of asset. The U.S. version of the leverage rule for the largest bank holding companies, known as the

Supplementary Leverage Ratio (SLR), now requires these firms to have a minimum ratio of capital to total assets of 5%, regardless of the risk composition of their assets. (The bank subsidiaries of these holding companies must meet a 6% minimum leverage ratio.) Intermediation of lowrisk assets is typically less profitable than intermediation of high-risk assets. Faced with the SLR, these largest U.S. bank holding companies are cutting back significantly on the intermediation of some lower-risk assets. For example, the ratio of risk-weighted assets to total assets for these largest banks has grown since 2013 from 55% to about12 65%. Appendix 1 provides additional discussion of the distortions in asset composition of bank balance sheets caused by the SLR.

The SLR has especially impaired the market for government-securities repo intermediation. Per unit of gross assets, repo intermediation of government securities has extremely low risk and low profit margins per unit of assets. This suggests that the economic force underlying this decline in repo intermediation is a variant of what Myers (1977) called "debt overhang," explained as follows.

On a typical repo intermediation trade, a bank-affiliated dealer lends cash to a counterparty who secures the loan with bonds, say treasuries. (The trade is not a loan in a legal sense, but amounts in effect to a secured loan.) The treasuries received by the dealer are then usually financed by the dealer itself on another repo, typically at a lower financing rate. The dealer profits from the difference between the two repo rates. Absent capital requirements, this repo intermediation trade is almost self-financing because the dealer passes the cash from one counterparty to the other, and the treasuries in the opposite direction. If a counterparty fails, the position can be liquidated with very low risk to the dealer because it is almost fully secured or over-secured by cash or safe treasuries. This trade causes almost no increase in the risk of the dealer's balance sheet. When required by the leverage rule to have significantly more capital for this trade despite the extremely low risk, the dealer's creditors benefit from the improved safety of their claims. The legacy shareholders therefore must suffer from a transfer of market value to the creditors. In effect, this debt overhang implies a "rental fee" for space on the dealer's balance sheet, equal to the wealth transfer from shareholders to creditors for the use of that space. In order for a trade to benefit the dealer's shareholders, the profit on the trade must exceed the rental fee for balance-sheet space.

Making Derivatives Markets Safer
Reducing the systemic risk of derivatives markets is also a work in progress. In the U.S., the majority of standard over-the-counter derivatives are now centrally cleared by regulated clearing houses. 30 The EMIR central clearing mandate is coming into force in Europe, beginning in June 2016 with certain types of interest-rate swaps. (A significant fraction of new interest rate swaps were already being centrally cleared. 31) Central clearing improves the transparency of counterparty risk and should, in principle, reduce default contagion risk. The successful migration of a large fraction of swaps into clearing houses, known as central counterparties (CCPs), will be one of the most impressive accomplishments of the financial reform program. I will also discuss slow progress with swap trade-data repositories, some improvements in derivatives markets exposures, and the general weakness of regulations of the huge and systemically important market for deliverable foreign exchange derivatives.

Clearinghouse Failure Risk A consequence of the big success in moving swaps into clearing house is that the largest CCPs have themselves become too big to fail. These CCPs are now undergoing reviews of their default management and recovery plans, regarding their compliance with CPMI-IOSCO principles for financial market infrastructure. 32 Regulatory stress tests of the resiliency of CCPs are contemplated at the level of local market regulators, but there is not yet an agreed global framework for stress testing. 33 In April 2016, ESMA published the results of its first annual CCP stress tests, based on its own stress criteria, and found34 that "the system of EU CCPs can overall be assessed as resilient to the stress scenarios used to model extreme but plausible market developments." Although statements of regulatory objectives for the failure resolution of CCPs are now generally in place,35 actionable plans and procedures for failure resolution have not yet been promulgated for comment, let alone put into place. This is contrary to the Key Attributes for Financial Market Infrastructure set out by the Financial Stability Board (2014).36 The FSB Resolution Steering Group's most recent survey of progress stated37 that "resolution frameworks for CCPs are not well developed. Systematic crossborder resolution planning processes are not yet in place for any of the largest CCPs although efforts are underway to establish such processes. The majority of respondents noted that their jurisdictions intend to develop or are still in the process of developing resolution regimes or policies for CCPs." In the United States, at least to my knowledge, no official-sector entity has even announced that it will take steps toward preparing its CCP administrative failure-resolution plans and procedures. Legal experts do not even agree on the applicability to CCPs of the Dodd-Frank's Orderly Liquidation Authority.38

 Mandating the central clearing of a vast amount of derivatives long before having an operating plan for the administrative failure resolution of systemically important CCPs represents an important deficiency in the financial-reform process. Trade Data Repositories Trade data repositories for derivatives have been set up and are now being populated with transactions data, but the resulting databases are not yet of much use for monitoring systemic risk. Slow progress in this area can probably be ascribed to (i) early regulatory uncertainty over how the data would be used effectively in practical financial-stability applications, (ii) some lack of systemic perspective, in the sense of the critique of post-regulatory reform offered by Claessens and Kodres (2014), and (iii) weak international coordination. There has not been a sufficiently clear distinction, in creating these vast new databases, between the two rather different classes of applications, which rely on two different types of data: 1. Bilateral outstanding counterparty exposures, by underlying asset class, before and after netting and collateral. Here, the greatest potential applications include monitoring risk flows through the network of key market participants, collateral usage, and counterparty risk mitigation practices, by asset type. Using data collected under the European Markets Infrastructure Regulation (EMIR), Abad, Aldasoro, Aymanns, D'Errico, Rousová, Hoffmann, Langfield, Neychev, and Roukny (2016) illustrate the potential usefulness of swap data repositories in this application area. 2. Transactions. Here, the greatest potential applications include: (i) posttrade price transparency, for the purpose of improving market competition, an issue discussed later in this report; (ii) investigation of financial misconduct such as insider trading or market manipulation

and (iii) conducting studies of the efficiency and stability of markets, for example diagnosing the causes and effects of "flash crashes." Separate from the construction of jurisdiction-level derivatives trade data repositories, the G20 Data Gaps Initiative (DGI) has triggered the construction of a relatively comprehensive and unified international data "hub," housed at the Bank for International Settlements. The Staff of the IMF and the FSB Secretariat (2015) explains how this data hub will include a unified, granular, and relatively comprehensive financial-stability database, with a special focus on the soundness and exposures of globally systemically important banks (G-SIBs). Phase 2 of the DGI, about to commence, will incorporate a focus on systemic inter-linkages, and has the promise of linking jurisdiction-level derivatives data so as to permit a more systemic perspective on financial stability in the derivatives market, and beyond.39 Until the jurisdiction-level trade data repositories are better constructed and can be used in a linked manner, the promise of the derivatives datarepository initiative will remain substantially unfulfilled. Regulatory Pressure to Reduce Swap Exposures The pressure of capital and liquidity requirements and soon-to-beimplemented minimum margin requirements for the swaps of dealers has significantly reduced swap exposures, and will continue to reduce them. Figure 5 shows that the total gross market value of outstanding swap

Regulatory Pressure to Reduce Swap Exposures The pressure of capital and liquidity requirements and soon-to-beimplemented minimum margin requirements for the swaps of dealers has significantly reduced swap exposures, and will continue to reduce them. Figure 5 shows that the total gross market value of outstanding swap positions is now less than half of its peak 2007 level. The vast majority of swaps still have a major bank-affiliated dealer on at least one side of the trade. Because of regulation, these dealers have a much lower incentive to maintain large swap portfolios than they did before 2007. Although the latest BIS triennial derivatives transactions-volume data will not be released until later in 2016, data gathered from trade repositories by ISDA (2016b) suggest that total swap transactions volumes have been relatively steady over the last several years, just as total gross market values have declined. This represents an important improvement in the efficiency of counterparty risk management and collateral use.

This improvement in exposure efficiency could potentially be ascribed somewhat to central clearing, which has the ability to reduce exposures through netting across many clearing members. Achieving a reduction in swap exposures through central clearing is effective, however, only if a sufficiently large fraction of swaps are centrally cleared and if clearing is concentrated in relatively few clearing houses, as shown by Duffie and Zhu (2012). Otherwise, central clearing can actually increase total swap exposures. Because of the lack of well-coordinated data repositories, we are still unable to tell how much central clearing has helped or hurt, overall, on this dimension. 40 Recent work by Ghamami and Glasserman (2016), however, has cast some doubt on the capital and collateral efficiency of central clearing, to the extent that it has been implemented up to this point.

The greatest source of improvement in swap counterparty exposure efficiency is clearly due to "trade compression," by which redundant long and short positions involving multiple dealers are discovered via data sharing by dealers with special utilities. These compression utilities then algorithmically initiate trades that effectively cancel the redundant positions. By April 2016, the largest such service provider, TriOptima, reported41 that its compression service had effectively "torn up" a cumulative total of 784 trillion USD notional of redundant derivatives. ISDA (2015) shows the remarkable impact of compression activity on the amount of outstanding positions in the interest-rate swap market, which accounts for most of the compression. Trade compression is a private initiative that was not directly promoted by regulation. Indirectly, however, the pressure of regulatory capital and margin requirements has surely been responsible for a substantial increase in beneficial trade compression. Foreign Exchange Derivatives "Deliverable" foreign exchange (FX) derivatives, those involving an exchange of one currency for another, represent as much systemic risk as any class of derivatives other than interest-rate swaps. Nevertheless, deliverable FX derivatives remain only lightly regulated. The U.S. Treasury Department exempted FX derivatives from key Dodd-Frank regulations involving margin, central clearing, and platform trading. The explanations offered by the U.S. Treasury for this exemption were based heavily on the notion that FX derivatives entail a small amount of counterparty risk. This suggestion is simply not correct, as I have documented. 42 Changes in the market values of deliverable FX derivatives during their lifetimes represent a systemically large amount of counterparty risk, unless safely margined. The U.S. has no current or proposed regulation of these instruments for central clearing, initial margin, or variation margin. Data provided by the Foreign Exchange Committee (2016) show a monthly transactions volume of $8.5 trillion of FX derivatives, the majority of which are for maturities of greater than one month, and with a high degree of concentration in individual currency pairs, especially Euros versus US dollars. FX derivatives involving the U.S. dollar account for about half of all trade. In Europe, EMIR has not designated deliverable FX derivatives for central clearing or initial margins, but will require the exchange of variation margin, 43 a big improvement over the stance of U.S. regulations. Deliverable FX derivatives are more difficult to regulate than conventional derivatives because they involve the exchange of two actual currencies. This requires international coordination, which has been lacking, 44 or raises "extra-territoriality" concerns. FX derivatives are also operationally more costly to regulate, again because of the need to handle different currencies. Meanwhile, FX derivatives markets represent a major source of systemic risk that is significantly under-regulated.

Improving Trade Competition The second central aim of the regulatory reform is to improve the competitiveness of financial markets, with a focus on off-exchange trading. The legacy structure of over-the-counter (OTC) markets has represented an inefficiently low degree of competition, as I will explain. To the extent that financial-stability regulations have reduced the incentives of bank-affiliated dealers to make markets, regulations in support of price transparency and competitive trading venues can mitigate losses in market liquidity. Some markets could become even more liquid once dealer intermediation of OTC markets is supplanted with more all-to-all anonymous trade competition. Here, the biggest pre-reform deficiencies were related to price transparency and direct competitive bidding for trades, both of which aid price discovery and the ability of investors to conduct effective low-cost comparison shopping. The result should be deeper and more liquid markets, lower execution costs, and better allocative efficiency. Appendix 2 explains why predominantly bilateral trade is uncompetitive and inefficient. Beginning in 2003, the U.S. had already brought post-trade price transparency into its corporate and municipal bond markets with its TRACE initiative. The Dodd-Frank Act has instead aimed at the swap market. Standardized swaps have been designated for immediate and public transactions reporting and for trade on multilateral trading facilities (MTFs), known in U.S. regulation as swap execution facilities (SEFs). Japan has followed a course similar to that of the U.S., and has achieved roughly the same level of implementation Europe's Markets in Financial Instruments Directive (MiFID II) and proposed MIFIR implementing regulations are more ambitious in scope than U.S. trade-competition reforms, but are moving more slowly. Some important regulations are still being designed. Implementation of some of the most important rules, including mandates for trade on MTFs, has been repeatedly delayed, and at this point is not scheduled until early 2018. Europe's MiFID proposal covers a wider set of instruments, including corporate bonds, and seems likely to have a broader and more complex set of rules and exemptions. At least until recently, a lack of coordination between US and EU authorities has been an unfortunate impediment to reform. The U.S. Commodity Futures Trading Commission (CFTC) began quickly,48 but laid out aggressively extraterritorial rules that seemed to delay and hamper cooperation. The most contentious issues between the US and EU have been related to mutual recognition of CCPs and multilateral trading facilities. As noted by IOSCO (2015), market participants strongly support cross-border recognition of trading facilities and CCPs, given the alternative of heavy costs of market fragmentation. As I will explain, execution costs are lower if more market participants compete on the same platform. Further, as modeled by Duffie and Zhu (2012), multilateral netting at fewer CCPs reduces counterparty exposures and collateral requirements. Recently, the US and EU have been making more progress with mutual recognition.

Mandates for Trade on Exchanges and Trade Platforms In the U.S. and Japan, significant steps have been made toward pre-trade price transparency and competitive swap trading, especially through the migration of over-the-counter trade toward exchanges and multilateral trade facilities (MTFs). Until new regulations forced some trading onto multilateral trading facilities, most OTC trade was typically conducted by private bilateral negotiation between two dealers, or between a "buy-side" firm and a dealer. Now, more than two thirds of new trades in standardized interest-rate swap and credit default swap index trading in the U.S. is conducted on MTFs. Buy-side firms typically obtain their positions on MTFs at which more than one dealer responds to requests for quotes (RFQ). A significant fraction of inter-dealer trade is conducted on MTFs that use a central limit order book. The result is sometimes called a "two-tiered" market. In terms of improving competition and lowering trading costs to buy-side market participants, the reforms fall short by not bringing all wholesale market participants, including dealers and buy-side firms, together onto common trade venues using "allto-all" anonymous central limit order books. On an all-to-all central limit order book49 (CLOB), the best price quotes on the limit order book are transparent to all market participants and are simultaneously executable. For example, a buyer can choose the lowest of all of the simultaneously available quoted prices. This is the essence of effective pre-trade price transparency. Moreover, on an all-to-all CLOB, a buy-side firm has the option supply quotes to other market participants, thus offsetting some of its execution costs with the ability to both make and take quotes. Setting up CLOB venues is justified when trading activity is sufficiently broad spread and frequent to generate attention to trading opportunities by liquidity providers and to provide sufficient fee income to the venue operator. Unfortunately, even after the implementation of Dodd-Frank, buy-side firms tend to avoid trading swaps on existing CLOB platforms. An important impediment here is the practice known as "name give-up," by which the identity of the buy-side firm must be "given up" to whichever firm is allocated its trade. This leaves a buy-side firm with little control over leakage of information about its trading intentions, as explained by the Managed Funds Association (2015a). This means that buy-side firms are effectively encouraged to trade on RFQ-based MTFs. The average trading costs of buyside firms are therefore higher than would be the case without the practice of name give-up. Another important loss of market competition arises from the fragmentation of trade across many different trade platforms. Well-established economic theory implies that markets are more efficient and investors receive better pricing when more market participants compete for trade at the same venue. Most obviously, from the viewpoint of a quote seeker, the best price from among a small set of bidders is not as attractive as the best price available from an enlarged set of bidders. This is true even if the bids do not depend strategically on the size of the bidding population. For example, for a wouldbe seller of a financial asset, the highest of the first 5 prices drawn from a given pool of potential bid prices is not as high as the highest of the first 50 bid prices. Strategic competition among bidders further improves the best price available to the quote seeker. That is, a given bidder will compensate for an increase in the population of competing bidders by bidding more, being aware that a given bid price is less likely to be the highest price as the set of bidders is enlarged.50 Figure 6, from a study of bond trading platforms by Hendershott and Madhavan (2015) confirms the theoretically anticipated relationship between the number of dealers providing quotes on Market Axess, a corporate bond MTF, and the expected trading cost to the quote requester, controlling for other factors. Figure 6 shows that expected trading cost decline rapidly with the number of dealers providing quotes. As explained by ISDA (2016a), one of the causes of fragmentation has been the lack of harmonization between the EU and US, with respect to rules and mutual recognition of trading facilities. The Final Report of the IOSCO (2015) task force on cross-border regulation provides a range of examples and principles for "passporting," a form of mutual recognition.

Post-Trade Price Transparency
In any market format, competition is generally improved by fast and comprehensive post-trade transaction reporting. The quick public dissemination of transactions prices gives all market participants an indication of the prices at which trades may be available in the next short interval of time. Knowledge of the "going price" is a particularly important mitigant of the bargaining disadvantage of buy-side market participants, who generally have much fewer direct observations of trading encounters than do dealers Post-trade transaction reporting also allows buy-side investors to monitor and discipline the execution quality of their past trades by

comparing the prices that they obtained from a dealer with the prices that were obtained for other trades conducted elsewhere in the market at around the same time. A dealer, aware of being monitored in this fashion through post-trade price dissemination, and at risk of losing reputation and repeat business over poor execution prices, will provide somewhat better pricing to its customer. Post-trade price transparency was mandated for the U.S. corporate bond market beginning in 2002, in the form of the Transaction Reporting and Compliance Engine (TRACE). This eventually lead to the public reporting of trade prices for essentially all U.S. corporate bonds and some other fixedincome instruments. TRACE has lowered bid-ask spreads in most of the segments of the bond markets that it covers, although the impact on market liquidity has not been uniformly positive, as explained in Appendix 3, which summarizes the empirical evidence on the impact of TRACE. Until post-trade transactions reporting is more effectively amplified by the full implementation of MiFID, buy-side participants in Europe's OTC markets will not have effective post-trade price transparency.

Appendix 1: SLR and Intermediation Distortions
Regulators are now requiring that a large bank's capital must exceed a given fraction of the bank's total quantity of assets, irrespective of their riskiness. This "leverage requirement" is simpler than the conventional risk-weightedasset (RWA) capital requirement, which calls for capital levels that depend on the average risk profile of the bank's asset portfolio. Conventional RWA capital rules had not worked well leading up to the Great Financial Crisis because the risks of some assets were badly understated. That's not so surprising for those assets whose riskiness is measured by banks themselves. Banks typically prefer lower capital levels than regulators would judge sufficient, and thus have a moral hazard to understate risks. Regulators, for their part, assign relatively undifferentiated

and unrealistically low risk weights to sovereign debt. Putting aside these incentive problems in setting risk weights, the risks are often difficult to estimate. The simplicity of the new leverage requirement, which treats all assets as though equally risky, has thus promoted its heavy use in new capital rules, to the point that the balance-sheet management of some of the largest banks seems to be determined in significant part by these new gross leverage requirements. This has implied a shift by some large banks away from low-risk low-profit intermediation, consistent with modeling by Kiema and Jokivuolle (2014). Models in which both banks and regulators are averse to risk-taking by banks, developed by Kim and Santomero (1988), Rochet (2008), and Glasserman and Kang (2014), show that "flattening" regulatory risk weights across asset classes, relative to actual risks, could inefficiently distort risk taking by banks, causing them to shift from low-risk assets to high-risk assets. This is not a surprise. Kiema and Jokivuolle (2014) also show that the leverage ratio rule can reduce financial stability by causing more banks to be jointly vulnerable to similar high-risk assets, unless the minimum leverage ratio pushes capital levels much higher. Debt overhang may be an even greater source of distortion in intermediation incentives under the supplementary leverage ratio. Debt overhang, a concept due to Myers (1977), refers to the incentive for a firm to avoid positive-net-present-value investments when the additional capital required for the investment causes a sufficiently large transfer in value from shareholders to creditors, due to a safer balance sheet. When a bank issues equity in order to meet a high regulatory capital requirement for a low-risk position, thus making its balance sheet safer, bank creditors benefit from a transfer of wealth through the increased safety of their debt claims. For such an intermediation trade to be economically viable, its mark-to-market profit must exceed the associated wealth transfer to creditors, as modeled by Andersen, Duffie, and Song (2016). Debt overhang is smaller for more highly capitalized banks, therefore giving them an important advantage in competing for trades. A natural reformation of risk-weighted capital requirements would make some differentiation across asset classes based on risk, but be conservative. An improved approach would recognize that, other things equal, banks are likely to invest more heavily in assets with lower risk weights. Even for an asset class that is fairly judged to be quite safe, concentrated investment increases the likelihood, given a bank failure, that this asset class is responsible for much of the loss. So, the lowest risk weights should not be as low as they are today. Moreover, as a bank's investments become more concentrated in a given asset class, the associated risk weights for that asset class should go up. The same principle applies on a systemic basis. As investments by banks, in aggregate, become more concentrated in a given asset class, risk weights for that asset class should rise. Further, assets whose risks are difficult to judge should be assigned higher risk weights. If an extreme-scenario loss is heavily model dependent, and if we are uncertain about which to model use, one should apply a model that is likely to be relevant contingent on the event of a large loss. When in doubt regulators should be more conservative. I now offer an simplified illustration of the debt-overhang impact of the SLR on the incentive of a bank to conduct a repo intermediation. 52 Consider a bank acting as a securities dealer, possibly through an affiliate subject to consolidated capital requirements under the Basel G-SIB standards. For simplicity, suppose that the SLR is binding for this bank, so that it must have at least C in additional capital for each additional unit of measured assets, regardless of the asset risk. On a candidate repo trade, the bank would initially receive from its counterparty German government bonds (bunds) with a market value of 1+H, in exchange for 1 in cash, where H is a "haircut" designed to protect the bank from counterparty failure. At maturity in one day, the bank returns the bunds to the counterparty in exchange for 1+R, where R is the repo rate, measured for simplicity on a per-day (rather than annualized basis). The repo rate R exceeds the bank's cost of funding by some rate spread G. In this case, the bank can obtain funding in the repo market by using the same bunds as collateral.

Repos are exempt from stays at counterparty failure, so the bank could suffer an unexpected loss on this trade only if, within a day, both of two unusual events happen: (i) the counterparty defaults and (ii) the value of the bunds drops by more than the haircut H. In practice, this combined outcome is so unlikely that an event of this type has not been reported since the 1982 failure of Drysdale Government Securities, when counterparties had mistaken their haircut assignments.53 So, in the absence of capital requirements, because this trade is nearly risk free trade, it has essentially no effect on the market values of the bank's debt and equity, other than the intermediation gain of G, which we can assume for simplicity is paid to equity as a distribution. Because the SLR is binding, however, the bank must have approximately C in additional equity in order to conduct this trade. A simple way for the bank to arrange this additional equity is to retire approximately C worth of unsecured debt, funded by an equity issuance of the same amount. In practice, the bank would not conduct an equity issuance for each repo trade. Instead, it would have a policy for how much repo it wishes to conduct on a normal on-going basis, and adjust its capital structure so as to meet its capital requirements, with some buffer designed to conservatively avoid compliance problems

In our simple example, the remaining legacy unsecured creditors benefit to the extent that the retired debt no longer claims a share of the recovery value of the bank's assets in the event that the bank defaults. Instead, that

default-contingent recovery claim is absorbed by the remaining unsecured creditors. The market value of this additional default-contingent debt recovery claim, per unit of retired debt, is the difference D between the market value of a default-free debt claim and the market value of an unsecured debt claim on the bank. This difference D is therefore equal to the credit spread S of the bank's unsecured debt. Because C units of debt were retired, the net gain in value to the legacy debt is therefore CS. Given that the balance sheet of the bank is otherwise unchanged, the shareholders' net gain is the funding spread G on the repo trade, less the wealth transfer of CS to legacy unsecured creditors. Thus, the incremental impact of the capital requirement on the bank's incentive to conduct the repo is equal to CS

For illustration, consider an SLR of 3% (the current European minimum regulatory leverage ratio for the largest EU banks) and a typical annualized bank credit spread of 100 basis points. 54 The bank must therefore lower its bid and raise its offer for bund repo intermediation by CS = 3 basis points each in order to compensate shareholders for the effect of SLR,55 for a total impact on the bid-offer spread of 6 basis points (bp). According to the ICMA European Repo Council (2015), "Historically, for short-dated liquid repo markets, typical bid-ask spreads would be less than 5bp, and possibly only 1-2bp." So, the impact of the SLR on repo intermediation incentives is bigger than the entire pre-SLR bid-ask spread. The International Capital Markets Association (ICMA) European Repo Council (2015) states that the leverage ratio rule is a major friction in the provision of repo intermediation by European banks. In terms of the impact of the SLR on repo market liquidity, however, Europe has the benefit over the United States, of (i) a lower SLR, (ii) an active direct-repo electronic platform trading market, and (iii) some broad-market central clearing of repos. I have already described the dramatic reduction in volume, and enormous increase in bid-ask spread, in the U.S. government securities repo market, since the imposition of the 5% SLR on the largest U.S. bank-affiliated broker-dealers. As far as the actual total quantity of repos conducted in Europe (whether by EU or non-EU banks), the latest survey of the EU repo market by the International Capital Markets Association (2016) shows little change in volume over the four-year period ending December 2015. The direct-repo market accounts for over half of all European repo trade.56 However, most European repo intermediation, even on direct-repo platforms, is done by banks. The market may someday evolve to one in which nonbank participants could offer significant direct repo intermediation, thus returning some liquidity to the market. Europe's CCP advantage should allow some European banks to net some of their long and short positions so as to reduce their measured repo assets. 57 That is, a bank doing matched-book repo intermediation with counterparties on both sides that clear through the same CCP can reduce its asset position by netting its long and short positions at the CCP, thus reduce its regulatory capital requirement for conducting repo intermediation, and therefore narrow its required bid-offer spread. As I have mentioned, the initiatives to begin a broad-market repo CCP in U.S. have not yet succeeded. Why Bilateral Trade is Often Inefficient In an opaque bilateral over-the-counter (OTC) market, two buy-side firms are rarely if ever be able to identify each other as beneficial direct trade counterparties. Almost invariably, a buy-side firm has no reasonable option but to trade with a dealer. In order to conduct a trade in the bilateral OTC market, a representative of a buy-side firm would typically contact a dealer's trading desk and ask for bid and offer quotes. The quotes are good only when offered, and only for trade sizes up to a conventional notional quantity that can depend on the type of product. The buy-side representative can either agree immediately to trade at the dealer's bid or offer, or can decline. If the buy-side firm agrees, then an increase in the notional quantity may also be negotiated. The dealer may agree to increase the notional quantity of the trade at the same price terms or may demand additional price compensation for increasing the size of the trade. This "bilateral" (one-on-one) trade negotiation places a buy-side firm at a substantial bargaining disadvantage to a dealer. A buy-side firm rarely has as much information as the dealer concerning the "going price" for the specific product. Thus, when offered given price terms by a dealer, a buy-side firm cannot be confident whether the dealer's quotes are near the best available quotes in the market. The buy-side firm does not know, moreover, which dealers are likely to provide the best quotes for the trade in question. As opposed to a dealer, a buy-side firm seeking to sell cannot obtain better pricing by trading directly with another buy-side firm that has a natural motive to buy, and vice versa. Moreover, a buy-side firm cannot force two or more dealers to compete effectively against each other for the trade because of the bilateral nature of the bargaining encounter. I will now elaborate on this last point. A buy-side firm has the option to reject the price terms quoted by the dealer with whom it is negotiating, and search for better terms from another dealer. But the buy-side firm must negotiate with dealers sequentially, that is, one at a time. The buy-side firm cannot choose the best from among various different dealers' simultaneously executable quotes. The mere fact that a buy-side investor can eventually request quotes from different dealers does not in itself cause dealers to compete aggressively with each other in order to win the investor's trade. In this setting of one-on-one negotiation, a buy-side market participant has no ability to force dealers to compete directly with each other. When facing a buy-side customer, each dealer holds a degree of monopoly power over its buy-side customer because the customer has no ability to pick the best of many simultaneously executable price quotes.58 In some cases, a buy-side firm would contact one or more dealers only to discover that the quoted prices are not sufficiently attractive, and would decline to trade at all. Because of the low degree of competition in the OTC market, the buy-side firm may have missed the opportunity to make a beneficial trade that might have been available at sufficiently attractive price terms in a more competitive market, such as that provided by an exchange. Missed opportunities for beneficial trade represent an additional cost of an opaque OTC market. When providing quotes in the OTC market, a dealer provides bid and ask prices that trade off the impact of widening the quoted bid-ask spread on (a) the profit that would result from agreement by the buy-side firm and (b) the probability of agreement. Widening the bid-ask spread increases the former and reduces the latter, because a wider quote increases the incentive of the buy-side firm to search for more favorable terms from another dealer (or to simply decline to trade). If the dealer perceives that the buy-side firm does not have an attractive "outside option" to search for other quotes, the dealer can widen its bid-ask spread accordingly. In a dealer-dominated opaque OTC market, the buy-side firm's outside option is a costly delay to find another suitable dealer, followed by another negotiation with a new dealer who has a bargaining position of similar strength to that of the first dealer contacted. There is no opportunity to get the two dealers (or more than two dealers) to bid directly against each other. The poor outside options available to buy-side firms in an opaque market therefore imply wider bid-ask spreads than would be available on an exchange. This discourages some trade, and the associated gains from trade are lost, a reduction in welfare. A significant experiment with post-trade price transparency was the introduction, mandated by the SEC beginning in 2002, of the Transaction Reporting and Compliance Engine (TRACE), which eventually lead to the public reporting of trade prices for essentially all U.S. corporate bonds and certain other fixed-income instruments. This appendix summarizes the empirical evidence of the impact of TRACE post-trade price transparency on the liquidity and competitiveness of U.S. corporate bond trading. Bessembinder and Maxwell

(2008) reported that "The introduction of transaction price reporting for corporate bond trades through the TRACE system in 2002 comprised a major shock to this previously opaque market. Investors have benefited from the increased transparency through substantial reductions in the bid-ask spreads that they pay to bond dealers to complete trades. Conversely, bond dealers have experienced reductions in employment and compensation, and dealers' trading activities have moved toward alternate securities, including syndicated bank loans and credit default swaps. The primary complaint against TRACE, which is heard both from dealer firms and from their customers (the bond traders at investment houses and insurance companies), is that trading is more difficult as dealers are reluctant to carry inventory and no longer share the results of their research. In essence, the cost of trading corporate bonds decreased, but so did the quality and quantity of the services formerly provided by bond dealers." Bessembinder, Maxwell, and Venkataraman (2006) found that with the introduction of TRACE, trade execution costs fell by about 50% for those bonds whose transactions were covered by TRACE. They also found a spillover effect: Even for bonds not covered at that time by TRACE transactions costs dropped by 20%. The authors speculate that publishing the prices of TRACE-eligible bonds provided additional information on the fair market values of bonds not eligible for TRACE reporting. Harris and Piwowar (2007) also find that TRACE reduced transactions costs. Goldstein, Hotchkiss, and Sirri (2007), however, find that less frequently traded bonds, and very large trades, showed no significant reduction in bidask spread with the introduction of public transaction reporting under TRACE. Moreover, Goldstein, Hotchkiss, and Sirri (2007) and Asquith, Covert, and Parath (2014) do not find that TRACE increased trading activity. Indeed, Asquith, Covert, and Parath (2014) found that TRACE reduced trading activity significantly for high-yield bonds. A reasonable interpretation is that, with the reduced profitability of market making caused by greater price transparency, dealers had a reduced incentive to make markets, especially in thinly traded bonds. Bessembinder and Maxwell (2008) note the dramatic increase in corporate bond trading volume on the electronic platform, MarketAxess, that followed the introduction of TRACE, saying, "We believe that TRACE improved the viability of the electronic market. In the presence of information asymmetries, less-informed traders will often be dissuaded from participating in a limit order market, knowing that their orders will tend to be 'picked off' by better-informed traders if the price is too aggressive, but left to languish if not aggressive enough. TRACE likely increased traders' willingness to submit electronic limit orders by allowing traders to choose limit prices with enhanced knowledge of market conditions." While bid-ask spread is often a useful measure of trading costs, Asquith, Covert, and Parath (2014) focus on intra-day price dispersion. The relevance of this measure is motivated by the idea that, in an opaque OTC market, the same bond, on the same day, can be traded by dealers at much different prices with some customers than with other customers, even if there has been no significant new fundamental information on the bond's quality during the day. Asquith, Covert, and Parath (2014) showed that the intraday dispersion of prices for riskier corporate bonds was reduced on average by over 40% with the introduction of TRACE post-trade price transparency for those bonds. This represents a dramatic reduction in effective trading costs for those buy-side investors who, without TRACE transparency, had been paying far higher trading costs than other (presumably more sophisticated and better informed) market participants.

Initial margin

The requirement for financial institutions to calculate dynamic initial margin is driven mainly by regulation. In

2017 the European Banking Authority (EBA) launched its Targeted Review of Internal Models (TRIM) project to assess whether the models currently used by banks comply with regulatory requirements and whether their results are reliable. TRIM states that banks need to capture time dependent initial margin for both cleared and non-cleared trades in line with "contractual arrangements."

In this blog, we will be discussing the problem of calculating dynamic initial margin in the context of counterparty credit risk. We will also look at some innovative solutions to this problem that the financial engineering research group at IBM have been investigating.

The definition of initial margin

Margin is defined as the amount that the holder of a financial instrument must deposit, either with their counterparty or exchange, to cover the risk associated with the instrument. Variation margin covers day-to-day changes in the instrument mark-to-market value and initial margin covers potential losses in the event of counterparty default. The term "initial" can be misleading, implying that the collateral is posted only at trade inception while the variation margin is posted day-on-day as the mark-to-market value of the trade changes. In fact, the amount of initial margin posted can vary day-on-day as well.

The calculation of initial margin

There are two main approaches used for the calculation of Initial Margin: a historical VaR (Value at Risk) simulation approach and a formulaic sensitivity-based approach that has been developed by ISDA (the International Swaps and Derivatives Association). This sensitivity-based approach is referred to as the Standard Initial Margin Model (SIMM).

Initial margin as a component of counterparty credit risk

Why do we need to calculate forward/dynamic initial margin?

Both front office traders interested in calculating pricing adjustments such as CVA (Credit Valuation Adjustment), and risk managers interested in monitoring the bank's exposure to its counterparties using measures such as PFE (Potential Future Exposure), will need to take account of initial margin through time. This initial margin forecast through time is referred to as forward or dynamic initial margin. The result is that if we are using the historical VaR approach to calculate initial margin in the context of counterparty credit risk, then we have hugely increased the computational burden. This is illustrated in the diagram below: each of the blue lines represents one of the market data scenarios (or paths) used to calculate credit risk. At each of the timesteps along these paths the red lines represent the nested historical simulation that must be carried out to determine the initial margin.

initial margin (IM) requirements are a global regulatory regime intended to limit systemic contagion by offsetting losses if an OTC derivatives counterparty defaults.

IM has significant implications for market participants' risk and collateral management operations, as well as their technology systems.

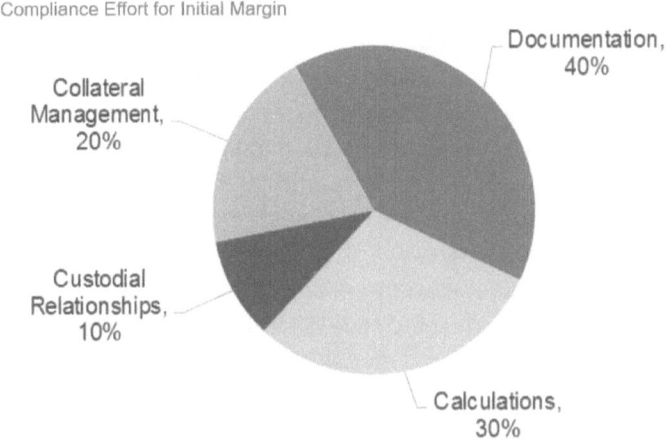

Documentation,
40%

Collateral
Management,
20%

Custodial
Relationships,
10%

Calculations,
30%

The standard practice in option pricing is to calibrate models to market prices of liquid instruments. Consequently all models (with enough degrees of freedom) will give the same price for standard options. Nevertheless, due to the different hypotheses implicit in the different models, the risks inferred will be different. As the most used risk measure, the first order sensitivity or out-of-the-model delta (or simply delta) will be the focus of this paper. The second order sensitivity or out-of-the-model gamma is also briefly discussed. There are certainly several places where it is mentioned that different models will lead to different risk numbers (in particular Rebonato [8]). This note does not present theoretically new developments but emphasizes the practical importance of model choice, even for simple and liquid instruments, for which the price is given by the market. The models studied are widely used in practice and actual figures are given reflecting the extent of the difference in risks. The first models analysed are the classical Black model for swaption (geometric Brownian motion of the forward swap rate) and its normal version (arithmetic Brownian motion of the forward swap rate). The next is the extended Vasicek (or Hull and White [4]; arithmetic Brownian motion of the continuously compounded rates) and its explicit formula for European swaptions [2]. The last three are stochastic volatility models based on a constant elasticity volatility (CEV) extension of Black model, known as SABR (stochastic, alpha, beta, rho)[1]. We use three versions of this model, one with the elasticity parameter β equal to 0 (normal), one with 1 (log-normal) and one with no correlation between rates and volatility ($\rho = 0$). For the Black, normal and Hull-White models we also compute the theoretical in-the-model delta equivalent and use the sensitivity of the underlying swap multiplied by this theoretical number. Moreover for the Black model, we compute the total delta and the delta coming from changing only the forward rate (no adjustment of the annuity or present value of a basis point). More details on the numerical procedures used are given in the Appendix. Troughout the paper the difference between normal-like or log-normal-like models is referred to as the market or model dynamic. It represents the fundamental market movements implied by each model's stochastic differential equation. The impact of model dynamic and market data (rate, smile, volatility level) are analysed separately. It is evident that the model dynamic is the dominant of the two impacts.

The different risk figures time series are provided in Section 4 for three models (Black, HullWhite and SABR with $\beta = 0$). The graphs clearly indicate the market parameters that influence the changes through time. Finally the real judgement arrives: the hedging contest. The game is simple: buy a ATM swaption each day, delta hedge it with each model and sell the swaption and its hedge the next day. This is done over several years. The best hedger is the model producing the smallest standard deviation of profit. And the winner of the contest is ... only announced at the end of the paper. The difference between the models is substantial. The choice of the model dynamic is an important decision that a risk manager has to take. The sensitivity dependency with regards to choosing the model is analysed in this section. The models described in the introduction are calibrated to ATM swaption For models with more freedom (SABR) the smile is calibrated at best to the smile as observed on that date The first (and main) risk measure analysed is the out-of-the-model delta to market rates For the Black, normal, and Hull-White models the sensitivity of the in-the-model delta equivalent is also analysed. The sensitivity of the underlying swap is computed and multiplied by that figure. Market dynamic. Different models have different probability distributions of the underlying, generating different price changes when the market moves (different sensitivities). This is often linked to the smile effect. This section shows that large sensitivity differences can appear even in absence of smile differences. Several versions of a model with different underlying dynamics are calibrated (very closely) to the same smile and still produce substantially different deltas. The models used is the SABR models with elasticity parameter (β) between 0 and 1. As an example, the figures are computed with a 10 million 1yx5y receiver at-the-money (ATM) swaption in USD on 25 June 2004. The prices are calibrated to ATM Black volatility of 23.5%, for the SABR model with 0 elasticity ($\beta = 0$, normal-like model), the (arbitrarily chosen) correlation (ρ) is 10% and the volatility of volatility (v) is 30%. The out-of-the-model yield curve deltas are reported in Table 5 for different tenors. The relative difference is computed with respect to the sensitivity of the underlying ATM forward swap. As can be seen from the numbers, the difference is close to 5% for a parameter of 0.5 and close to 10% for 1. The version of the model with elasticity 0 has the largest delta in absolute value. The yield curve gamma for ATM swaptions is also reported in Table 5. The impact of the dynamic depends on the swaption moneyness. The sensitivities of receiver out-of-the-money (OTM) swaptions are computed with different strikes (1, 2, and 3% below and above forward rate). The yield curve sensitivities (delta and gamma) are reported in Table 6

	β	0	0.25	0.50	0.75	1
Delta	Sensitivity	-2,257	-2,154	-2,052	-1,950	-1,848
	Difference	–	103	205	307	410
	Relative difference (%)	–	2.38	4.75	7.12	9.49
Gamma	Sensitivity	16.64	16.54	16.75	16.51	16.28
	Difference	–	-0.09	0.11	-0.13	-0.36
	Relative difference (%)	–	-0.57	0.64	-0.77	-2.14

moneyness and two different elasticity parameters. Relative difference for delta is with respect to the one of the swap and for gamma with respect to the one of the ATM swaption with $\beta = 0$. We have the same pattern with the 0 elasticity model giving a larger delta. The difference being between 0 and 5% of the risk of the underlying. The discrepancy is larger for the at-the-money than for out-the-money options. It may seem paradoxal that all pri

SIMM model
Each trade is allocated into a product class. There are 4 product classes in total: The margin for each risk class is defined as the sum of the Delta Margin, the Vega Margin, the Curvature Margin and the Base Correlation Margin.

• Interest Rates and FX (RatesFX)

• Credit

• Equity

• Commodity

Within each product class, risk is broken down into 6 risk classes:

Interest Rate

• Credit (Qualifying)

• Credit (Non-Qualifying)

• Equity

• Commodity

 • FX

The margin for each risk class is defned as the sum of the Delta Margin, the Vega Margin, the Curvature Margin and the Base Correlation Margin

SIMM is calculated for each product class taking into account correlations across risk buckets within risk classes.

Total SIMM is the IM of all the product classes combined after applying concentration addons/multipliers.

What-if calculations are not enough

Though they are still very useful for knowing your theoretical risk and reward conditions, the simple static scenario calculations from the previous article are not sufficient when you want to manage a long straddle position in real time. In this case, you will need to measure the position's exposure to major factors like underlying stock price or passing time at every moment.
Yes, we are now talking about the option Greeks. With today's option trading platforms you can watch the Greek values in real time summed up for your whole position and see the exposure immediately. Let's now look at the most important one: the delta.

Opening a long straddle position at the money

Let's say you have opened a long straddle position by buying a call and a put option on Bank of America, both options with strike price of 20. If Bank of America stock is trading at 20 at the time, both these options are at the money. This is when a long straddle position can be bought for the lowest price and when it makes the most sense to open it if you intend to play it as an unbiased non-directional long volatility trade.

Long straddle delta at the money is zero

An at the money call option has a delta of roughly 0.50 (if stock price goes up 1 dollar, the call option's price goes up by 0.50), while an at the money put option has a delta of roughly -0.50 (if stock price goes up 1 dollar, the put option's price goes down by 0.50). If you hold both options simultaneously, the total delta of your position is the sum of the two deltas, which in this case equals zero. This is in line with long straddle being a non-directional trade.

Stock goes up from the strike price: delta turns positive

If Bank of America stock price goes up by several dollars, the call option you hold as part of the straddle is now in the money and its delta increases to somewhere between 0.50 and 1.00. The put option on the contrary is out of the money (if the stock ended up higher than the strike price, the put option would be worthless at expiration). The put option's delta moves closer to zero and it is now somewhere between -0.50 and zero.

You again calculate the total long straddle delta by summing up the two deltas (a larger positive number for the call and a smaller negative number for the put). You get a positive number. For example the call option's delta is 0.70, the put option's delta is -0.30, and the total long straddle delta is 0.40. As a result of the underlying stock price going up, the long straddle position has become directional. It has a positive delta and its value and your profit increases as the stock price goes up.

The higher the stock, the higher the delta

The higher the underlying stock price gets:

- the higher the call option delta is (closer to 1.00),
- the closer the put option delta is to zero, and

- the higher (more positive) the total long straddle delta is.

When the stock price gets very far from the straddle's strike and/or very little time remains till the straddle's expiration, the call option's delta is almost 1.00, the put option's delta is almost zero, and the long straddle position behaves almost like a long stock position.

An end-user with fixed and real (RPI-linked) risk exposures (liabilities, debt, market-making) will typically consider the following option strategies • Terminology tip: payer and receiver refers to the position of the option buyer with respect to the fixed or real leg. – the buyer of a payer (interest rate) swaption has an option to pay a fixed rate (the strike) and receive a floating rate LIBOR – the buyer of an inflation receiver has an option to receive a fixed rate and pay RPI – the buyer of a real rate receiver has an option to receive the real rate (the strike) and pay a floating rate LIBOR

Monetize triggers	Sell interest rate or real rate payer Sell inflation receiver
Tail-risk hedging	Buy interest rate or real rate receiver Buy inflation payer
Risk management	Buy and sell payers and receivers

Monetizing inflation-hedging triggers

End user :UK Pension Scheme

Client Requirement : Client wished to monetise a trigger to hedge (RPI) inflation at 3.2% by selling away the opportunity to benefit from a fall in RPI inflation below 3.2%.

Actions :

Sold an (RPI) inflation receiver swaption. –

Underlying was a zero coupon (RPI) inflation swap

- Strike rate was ATMF-30bps (Forward starting RPI base)

2y5y/10y/30y/50y - large (underlying swap PV01)

- Swap settled, collateralized with third party valuations

Pension funds need to hedge the interest rate risk of the liabilities. To do this, several alternatives exist. One of them is hedging by swaptions. However, the application of this strategy can be performed through a buy and hold swaption strategy or a dynamic delta replicating strategy. As the implied volatility in the swaption market may overreact to some market circumstances and swaptions may be priced for insurance properties it provides, it might be worth to replicate the swaption. This research has been done to compare the swaption strategy with the dynamic delta replicating strategy. This is done by using historical data. The simulations for this research are based on different costs structures and different rebalancing periods. Trading costs of dynamic delta replicating strategy overtakes the swaption trading costs. Saving trading costs is possible by decreasing the rebalancing frequency. The counter effect is the increase of the hedging error. After giving information about the periodical development of the strategies, the comparison of the strategies is done for results at expiry date of each analyzed swaption. The difference between the results of both strategies is affected by implied volatilities and the direction of the underlying interest rate move. This is best observed in the simulations of the crisis period. To complete the research, individual scenarios are analyzed.

Delta-Hedging

The so called delta-hedging is a dynamic hedging strategy. Here, it is sought, price changes of the swap to be compensated with price changes of the swaption. This is achieved by setting up a portfolio by holding (or shorting) the derivative (swaption) and shorting (or holding) a quantity Δ of the underlying (swap); this is referred to as hedge portfolio. In this way, within the portfolio, price increases of the swap are compensated by price drops of the swaption and vice-versa. Risks caused by fluctuations of the underlying security are practically eliminated. As can be verified, this portfolio has a delta of zero (let PPort be the price of the portfolio)

Therefore, by way of delta-hedging, one can eliminate (at least theoretically and to a great extent practically) the risk. The proportion of the underlying security in the portfolio must be continuously changed since the quantity Δ depends on both the price of the underlying and the remaining period to maturity of the swaption. This process is called dynamic hedging (or rebalancing) of the portfolio. Therefore (theoretically), one continuously has to buy and sell swaps. However, in the case of a discrete model, rebalancing of delta is done at discrete time intervals Δt

Servicing clients can require posting Initial Margin (IM) for client trades, and for their hedges. IM should be forecast for both and reflected in MVA. For non-vanillas with dynamic hedges, forecasting hedge-trade IM is challenging as future hedge ratios are necessary, and future sensitivities are difficult to compute. However, future sensitivities are already required to forecast client-trade IM, and thus future hedges (e.g., delta and vega) can be determined. In turn, this allows IM requirements to be forecast for cleared hedges (e.g., swaps) and non-cleared hedges (e.g., swaptions).

MVA Inclusive of All Associated IM Requirements This article operationalizes a definition of the Margin Valuation Adjustment (MVA) explicitly incorporating all sources of Initial Margin (IM). This section formalizes the potential sources of IM under typical hedge configurations and formulates the MVA definition accordingly. IM is certainly required for positions cleared with Central Clearing Houses (CCHs) and may be required for non-cleared positions, depending on the counterparty, and in such cases the IM amount is determined by the Standard Initial Margin Model (SIMM). MVA for client portfolios can be written as

$$\mathrm{MVA} = \mathrm{E}_{t_0}\left[\int_{t_0}^{T} e^{-D(t)}\,\mathrm{IM}(t)\,\phi_{\mathrm{IM}}(t)\,dt\right],$$

where ϕIM(t) is the funding spread for IM and D(t) is an integrated discounting rate that typically depends on the short rate and the hazard rates of the bank and its client. MVA is motivated in Green and Kenyon [7] as a necessary component of "total" valuation for client portfolios given that the funding of posted IM presents an additional cost to the bank in servicing a client. Naturally, IM due to hedging a client portfolio should contribute to MVA, as in e.g., Kenyon and Iida

Regarding MVA computation, Green and Kenyon [7] explore general regression-based methods, while Andersen and Dickinson [3] focus on cleared portfolios and develop analytical approximations. Antonov et al. [4] and Fries et al. [6] devise efficient methods for forecasting IM in cases where computing future SIMMIM is expensive (e.g. Bermudans)

These articles, along with that of Kenyon and Iida [10], compute MVA for a static set of trades, be they client trades or their hedges. As formalized momentarily, MVA for non-cleared non-vanillas such as Bermudans often requires that IM be forecast for dynamic hedging portfolios, comprised of cleared and non-cleared hedges. Developing a computational procedure for this challenging requirement is the key contribution of this article In realistic settings, client trades are hedged using combinations of instruments. Client trades may have one of the following arrangements; a) cleared, b) non-cleared with IM, or c) non-cleared but exempt from IM, e.g., for a genuine corporate "end user". Hedging portfolios will, in general, represent a mix of cleared and non-cleared positions, which covers both dynamic and static hedging strategies, including backto-back hedges. All non-cleared hedges are assumed to attract IM as they are positions with other financial institutions, which are "in-scope" for IM requirements. The general setup is captured in Figure 1

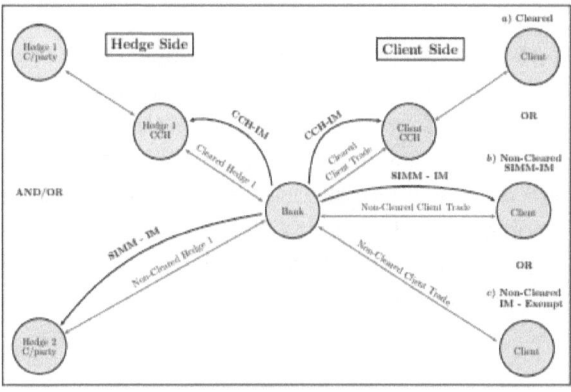

Figure 1: General hedging of a client-trade with potential IM requirements

The approach adopted here applies to trades involving multiple risk factors, represented as a vector R(t). It will however serve the exposition immensely to restrict focus to Interest Rate (IR) client trades involving only delta and vega risk factors. Let these be represented as $R_\Delta(t)$ and Rv (t), respectively, which can be interpreted as IR curves and IR volatility surfaces or cubes; gamma hedges etc., are ignored but could easily be accommodated. A useful example of such a trade is a non-cleared Bermudan swaption, given their liquidity and centrality to managing pre-payment risk of lending portfolios. A Bermudan client trade with a financial counterparty is an example of case b) in Figure 1 as SIMM-IM is applicable. Depending upon how well-developed the market for Bermudans is for a given currency, the hedge may involve more-liquid Bermudans. For example, a bespoke variable-notional Bermudan may be (partially) hedged with liquid constant-notional Bermudans. At this point it is assumed for simplicity however that hedges involve the most-liquid instruments possible, which are vanilla swaps and European swaptions, and that hedges are dynamically rebalanced. The possibility of hedging with Bermudans is treated in Section 3. In the setup used here, non-cleared European swaptions will hedge vega, attracting further SIMM-IM, and cleared vanilla swaps will hedge delta, attracting CCH-IM; in reality Europeans carry both delta and vega risk, but it eases the exposition to refer to such as vega hedges. To introduce notation, let IMc denote the IM attracted by the client trade, let IMh Δ i (t) denote the IM attracted by the ith delta-hedge counterparty, and let IMh v j (t) denote the IM associated with the jth vega-hedge counterparty. In practice, the delta-hedging swaps will be cleared, and thus IMh Δ i (t) will actually represent the IM attracted by the ith CCH. The "complete" MVA is

$$\mathrm{MVA} = \mathbb{E}_{t_0}\left[\int_{t_0}^{T} e^{-D(t)}\left(\underbrace{\mathrm{IM}^c(t)}_{\text{client}} + \sum_i \underbrace{\mathrm{IM}^{h_i^\Delta}(t)}_{\Delta\,\text{c/parties}} + \sum_j \underbrace{\mathrm{IM}^{h_j^\nu}(t)}_{\nu\,\text{c/parties}}\right)\phi_{\mathrm{IM}}(t)\,dt\right],$$

In recent years, banks have begun to charge FVA to clients for the funding costs inherent in (mainly uncollateralised) derivatives transactions. FVA has become synonymous with the more traditional (and less controversial) credit value adjustment (CVA). The work of Piterbarg (2010) and Burgard and Kjaer (2011) highlighted FVA from a theoretical viewpoint as the incorporation of the funding costs and benefits into the value of a derivatives transaction. The adoption of FVA has been reasonably swift and anecdotally it is seen in most market prices quoted to clients. Furthermore, FVA accounting adjustments have also been made in the financial statements of most major banks. Note that the question over FVA is interrelated with a similar question on the relevance of DVA. Arguments supporting FVA would tend to avoid DVA on the basis that it is already incorporated in the former as a funding benefit. Despite the quite rapid incorporation of FVA in pricing, some authors have questioned its validity, notably Hull and White (2012, 2014) and Andersen et al. (2016). These frameworks tend to support notions such as DVA and then conform to price symmetry and the law of one price. One way‡ to interpret these arguments is that FVA is merely an internal transfer of wealth within a firm and therefore should not need to be represented in that firm's financial statements. Even agreeing with this argument, there is still justification for a bank charging a client FVA. One example is that part of the funding cost should be charged in the form of a funding risk premium which is the component of the funding cost that is not related to the credit risk of the party concerned (Morini and Prampolini 2011). Hull and White (2014) support this by stating the FVA is "justifiable only for the part of a company's credit spread that does not reflect default risk". Andersen et al. (2016) also justify FVA from a pricing (but not accounting) perspective by showing that it arises from the maximisation of shareholder value. Since shareholders pay funding costs that represent a windfall to creditors in the event of default (Burgard and Kjaer 2011), an FVA charge in a transaction acts as a compensation to shareholders for this wealth transfer effect. Whether or not the presence of such charges in transaction prices justifies its use as an accounting adjustment remains a debate. Some would argue that the definition of fair value as an exit price under IFRS 13 does indeed support this notion. After all, a party's exit price is another party's entry price.

Not surprisingly, MVA represents similar problems to FVA in terms of its validity in pricing and as an accounting adjustment. As with FVA, Andersen et al. (2016) show that the overall effect of initial margin posting has no net impact on the total value of a firm and these authors therefore argue that it should not be a component of financial statements. However, analogously to FVA, charging MVA to a client can be justified from a shareholder-centric point of view that provides compensation for the wealth transfer. Hence, it seems likely that MVA will receive much attention in the coming years similar to recent interest in FVA. However, MVA differs from FVA for the following reasons:

• FVA charges are normally imposed directly on a client and relate to the actual transaction in question and the fact that the client is not (perfectly) collateralising that transaction. As such, FVA charges can often be determined without reference to other transactions. By contrast, initial margin requirements are generally only relevant between financial institutions who cannot charge each other. Traditional end-user clients are exempt from centrally clearing trades or posting initial margin bilaterally. § Hence, an MVA charge may not relate to an actual client transaction but rather to the hedge(s) that arise in order to neutralise the market risk of the transaction. For example, an end-user client may be charged CVA and FVA on the basis that they are (partially) uncollateralised but also an MVA due to the fact that the hedge of the transaction attracts initial margin requirements (either as a result of central clearing or the bilateral margin rules). • It has been argued (e.g. see Albanese 2015) that FVA can be reduced since regulatory capital can be used to fund variation margin payments. This argument would not apply to MVA since initial margin is pledged by title transfer and is therefore not interchangeable with capital. • Whereas FVA involves a wealth transfer between shareholders and creditors, the analogous MVA benefit applies only to creditors that benefit from initial margin, namely derivatives creditors. Hence, MVA should be seen as a wealth transfer to derivatives creditors from other creditors. This may in turn create agency problems where unsecured lenders may struggle to gauge the remuneration they require unless they understand to what extent they are subordinated to derivatives creditors in the event of a default. This paper will use a structural model to illustrate the latter point above showing the impact of initial margin posting on derivatives creditors and other creditors (termed generically as bondholders). This is important since regulatory changes such as the clearing mandate and bilateral margin requirements aim to reduce systemic risk via initial margin posting. However, whilst initial margin reduces the counterparty risk losses on derivatives trades, it increases losses of other claimants (Pirrong 2013). Whilst initial margin might therefore reduce systemic risk in derivatives markets (due to smaller default losses), it may increase it in these other markets where greater losses may have to be absorbed. 2.2 Liquidity impact of initial margin Initial margin aims to create a "defaulter pays" environment where a defaulted counterparty pays for claims a priori via pledging initial margin which is held in a segregated account (to prevent it being used for other purposes thereby increasing counterparty risk). Initial margin is a concept that developed on derivatives exchanges to cover the close-out costs of relatively short-dated and liquid transactions. When applied to OTC derivatives, the underlying maturity transformation that occurs is more stark as illustrated in Figure 1. This shows a five-year maturity transaction in situations without and with initial margin. Methodologies & Approximations for CCH-IM & SIMM-IM This section briefly recaps IM rules for cleared and non-cleared trades, and discusses associated computational techniques. Its purpose is to demonstrate that both flavors of IM can be evaluated via sensitivities. These will be exact for the non-cleared case but will involve approximations for the cleared case. The following section demonstrates how sensitivities of hedging positions can be inferred from those of client trades under reasonable assumptions on the hedging strategy. CCHs have long required parties to cleared trades to post IM in addition to Variation Margin (VM). VM is based on the current valuation of a portfolio, while IM is based on its risk over the Margin Period of Risk (MPoR). The MPoR is of short horizon, e.g., 10 days, and the risk measure used is typically a variant of a Value-at-Risk (VaR) for gains. VaR methodologies will be relevant throughout the article so some notation will be useful. The α-level δ-horizon VaR, Gα,δ(t), satisfies

$$\mathbb{P}_R(V(t, R(t + \delta)) - V(t, R(t)) < G^{\alpha,\delta}(t)) = \alpha \,,$$

If you leave it un-hedged you are exposed to the risk of large moves, especially when the option is at or near money. When you are deep out or deep in, Delta is flat and asymptotic as shown above. But when are you not, a large move can result in significant trading loss despite being Delta hedged. As long as prices move in small increments and do not jump dramatically, Delta hedge will cover you. The underlying jumps, you are exposed. We have seen this at work earlier with duration and convexity with similar implications. Delta is the first order rate of change and works well within a narrow band. Within and outside that band Gamma tracks not just the error but also the magnitude of your gain/loss in case of a large move (up/down). The magnitude of the error shifts dramatically as the option gets closer to the At/Near money state. When options are deep in or deep out, similar to Delta, Gamma also flattens out. However given the convex nature of the 2nd derivative in this case, the impact of a large up move or a large down move is not symmetric. But you can't hedge higher order Greeks (Gamma) by buying or selling the underlying. Why not? First the 2nd derivative of a spot/forward/linear position is zero so hedging Gamma through the underlying is out. The second complexity arises with Vega. We really don't know what shape or form realized volatility will take in the future. How can we effectively hedge it? Then there is the issue of term structure of volatility. Implied volatility changes based on time to maturity (term structure) as well as money-ness (deep in, deep out, At/Near – strike price) so taking a simple constant volatility view across all options irrespective of maturity or money-ness would actually be in-accurate The third catch is that both Gamma and Vega use exactly the same calculation function for Calls and Puts (Gamma for a call and put has the same value, Vega for a call and a put has the same value). Which creates interesting implications for hedging a book of options with calls and puts. You may be perfectly hedged and squared with respect to your Gamma and Vega exposures but the wrong universe/direction of hedging choices can still wipe you out. We hedge Gamma and Vega by buying other options (specifically cheaper out of money options) with similar maturities. Like Delta hedging we need to rebalance but the rebalance frequency is less frequent than Delta hedging. Your final hedge is therefore a mix of exposure to the underlying (partial delta hedge) and cheaper options with similar maturities. The only question is that it's a large universe of options out there, how do we manage multiple constraints including premium & sensitivities across products, maturities (tenors), Delta, Gamma & Vega. The answer is constraint optimization through Excel solver. Our first attempt to hedge higher order Greeks is a simple illustrative scenario with a single option contract. We start off where we stopped in **lesson one on hedging higher order Greeks**.

We have sold (written) a single position in a call option on NVIDIA (NVDA) on 14th May 2014. Our objective is to hedge Gamma and Vega exposure using a universe of cheaper options on the same date. Our model will essentially look for an optimal combination of cheaper options that completely or partially offset our Gamma and Vega exposure. Since we have sold (written) options we are short Gamma and Vega. Our offsetting position requires a trade that will be positive Gamma and Vega. The positive Gamma and Vega trade is possible when we buy options or pay the premium.

Here is the original option specification for the call option contract that has been written by our desk. Each contract that we write includes a bundle of 100 options. In our initial model and trial run we will solve for a single option and then scale the results for 100 contracts.

Option Contract Size	100	
Exposure to be hedged	100 X	
Option Specification	1	
Time to Expiry	1	
Strike Price	18.1	X
Option price	2.096	
Delta	0.56	
Gamma	0.076	
Vega	0.250	
Rho	0.081	
Theta	- 1.069	-

Figure 1 Hedging Greeks – Our short position

Of the above specification the two things of immediate interest to us are the option **premium ($2.1)** and the **expiry (1 year)**. Our hedge portfolio cannot cost more than $2.1 and while we can play with the expiry of our hedge portfolio we would ideally like to match it as much as possible with our short exposure.

Gamma and Vega exposures – Positive or negative?

Should you leave some residual Gamma and Vega exposure or should our hedging portfolio neutralize it in its entirety? From the fixed income and ALM world comes an interesting parallel. In the ALM world to preserve surplus or immunize capital from interest rate changes we match the weighted average of the first order sensitivity (modified duration) but we require that the second order sensitivity (convexity) of Assets is great than the convexity of liabilities.

Similarly in the options world while we may match Delta completely, we would aim to create a hedging portfolio with excess Gamma and Vega exposure compared to our original short position. If that is not possible we will let the positions run with the Gamma and Vega mismatch but use exposure limits to track our sensitivity to these two factors. Our hedge is going to be an imperfect semi-hedge which would leave some room for benefiting from unanticipated changes in market volatility as well as large unexpected jumps in the price of the underlying.

Hedging Higher Order Greeks – Structuring the problem.

The first question that comes up for discussion is that within the settings of Excel solver what objective function will we use to create our semi-perfect hedge. The objective function is the cell Solver will optimize. Since it is a single cell and we have two targets (Gamma and Vega exposure) we would need to be creative to structure a variable that will lead to exposure minimization under both the heads.

The second question revolves around the constraints we need to define an acceptable solution. We address both in this section.

Model design.

Our first step is to put aside the universe of options available for hedging. For our first round we limit the universe to call options. On 14th May 2014, there were around 104 call options that were available across the combination of maturities and strikes. The universe excludes 10 longer maturity options that we have selected for short positions.

We add a new column at the beginning of the universe titled **"Allocation"** which we will use in our solver model to allocate hedge portfolio weight to a given option contract.

Option Universe - Available for Hedging - Universe

Allocation	Date	Expiry	Expiry (Years)	Strike	Money-ness	C or P	Impl.
1%	05/14/14	720	2.00	28.96	60	C	0.
1%	05/14/14	30	0.08	19.005	5	C	0
1%	05/14/14	1080	3.00	23.53	30	C	0.
1%	05/14/14	1080	3.00	24.435	35	C	0.
1%	05/14/14	1080	3.00	27.15	50	C	0
1%	05/14/14	720	2.00	20.815	15	C	0.
1%	05/14/14	720	2.00	21.72	20	C	0
1%	05/14/14	1080	3.00	28.055	55	C	0.
1%	05/14/14	720	2.00	25.34	40	C	0.
1%	05/14/14	720	2.00	26.245	45	C	0
0%	05/14/14	30	0.08	18.100	0	C	
0%	05/14/14	720	2.00	27.15	50	C	0.
0%	05/14/14	720	2.00	28.055	55	C	0
0%	05/14/14	60	0.17	18.100	0	C	0.
0%	05/14/14	120	0.33	23.53	30	C	
0%	05/14/14	30	0.08	19.910	10	C	0

Figure 2 Option Hedging Universe – The selection of options available to hedge Gamma and Vega

d1	d2	N(d1)	N(d2)	Price	Delta	N'(d1)	Gamma	Vega	Rho	Theta
-0.97	-1.37	0.16	0.09	0.526	0.16	0.25	0.035	0.229	-0.05	0.46
-0.57	-0.65	0.28	0.26	0.242	0.28	0.34	0.237	0.065	-0.00	2.93
-0.27	-0.75	0.39	0.23	1.887	0.39	0.38	0.044	0.433	-0.16	0.60
-0.35	-0.83	0.36	0.20	1.692	0.36	0.38	0.043	0.423	-0.15	0.59
-0.57	-1.05	0.28	0.15	1.226	0.28	0.34	0.039	0.382	-0.12	0.53
-0.13	-0.52	0.45	0.30	1.960	0.45	0.40	0.055	0.360	-0.12	0.76
-0.24	-0.63	0.41	0.26	1.690	0.41	0.39	0.054	0.355	-0.11	0.74
-0.64	-1.12	0.26	0.13	1.102	0.26	0.33	0.037	0.367	-0.11	0.51
-0.63	-1.03	0.26	0.15	0.942	0.26	0.33	0.046	0.301	-0.08	0.61
-0.72	-1.12	0.23	0.13	0.815	0.23	0.31	0.043	0.283	-0.07	0.58
0.04	-0.03	0.52	0.49	0.566	0.52	0.40	0.282	0.077	-0.01	3.42
-0.81	-1.20	0.21	0.11	0.704	0.21	0.29	0.040	0.265	-0.06	0.54
-0.89	-1.29	0.19	0.10	0.609	0.19	0.27	0.038	0.247	-0.06	0.50
0.06	-0.05	0.52	0.48	0.793	0.52	0.40	0.202	0.110	-0.01	2.40
-1.50	-1.66	0.07	0.05	0.083	0.07	0.13	0.044	0.048	-0.00	0.59
-1.06	-1.14	0.15	0.13	0.112	0.15	0.23	0.146	0.040	-0.00	2.15

Figure 3 Adding Greeks to the Options Universe

Option Greeks are then used to calculate our hedge portfolio Greeks. For each of the Greeks in the table below the formula is a simple **sumproduct** of the hedge portfolio allocation weight and the Greeks in question. The first vector in the formula below is the portfolio allocation weight, the second is the Greek in question across the universe. The multiplier is the scaling factor that we will use later to scale results from 1 option contract to 100 contracts.

	fx	=SUMPRODUCT(B52:B158,R52:R158)*$H$6		

F	G	H	I
Portfolio Gamma	=SUMPRODUCT(B52:B158,R52:R158)*$H$6		
Portfolio Vega	0.04	82%	0.205
Portfolio Delta	0.05	91%	0.51
Portfolio Rho	0.01	85%	0.07
Portfolio Theta	- 0.16	85%	- 0.91
Portfolio Price	0.17	9%	1.93

Figure 4 Calculating Hedge portfolio metrics

Applying this formula for each of the Greeks give us the following table of hedge portfolio Greeks. We will use elements of this table in our model.

		Unhedged Limit	Unhedged Exposure
Portfolio Gamma		0.01	84%	0.0
Portfolio Vega		0.04	82%	0.2
Portfolio Delta		0.05	91%	0.5
Portfolio Rho		0.01	85%	0.0
Portfolio Theta	-	0.16	85%	- 0.5
Portfolio Price		0.17	9%	1.9

Figure 5 Hedging portfolio metrics

We have most of the components we need to setup the Solver model.

For our objective function we create a new cell titled Gamma-Vega-Unhedged which is the simple sum of Gamma Vega un-hedged exposure from the table above. Our first iteration solver model will aim to minimize this number. To ensure that we don't run into negative territory we will assume a non-negative model.

Portfolio Expiry	0.299	1	0.70
Gamma-Vega-Unhedged	0.269		

Figure 6 Solver objective function

In terms of constraints the first constraint we want to setup is to ensure that our average hedge portfolio expiry is less than the short position maturity. A second constraint would be to ensure that the hedge portfolio Gamma and Vega figures are atleast the same but ideally greater than the Gamma, Vega estimates for our short position.

Let go ahead and set up the model. To use the solver add-in click on the Data tab in Excel and chose the Solver add-in. If you don't see the Solver add-in please use the Excel setting to enable the add-in. The add-in is only available in the professional edition of Microsoft Office/Excel.

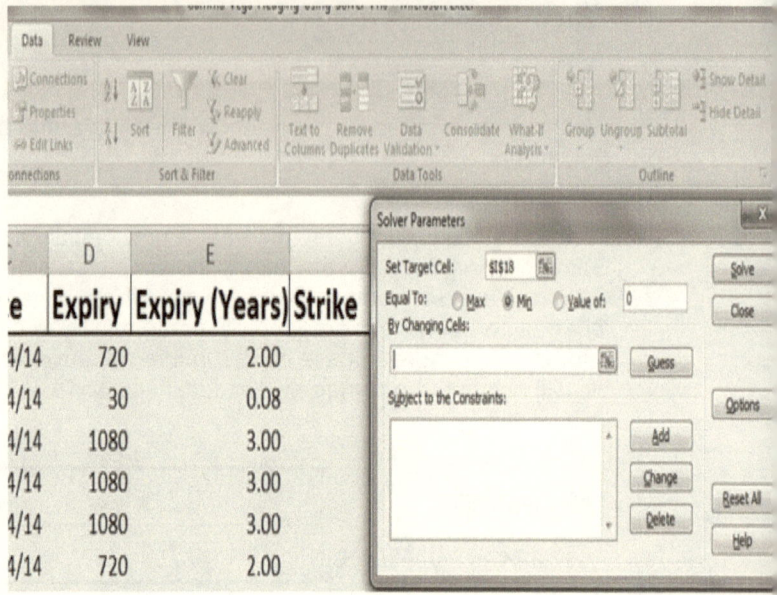

Figure 7 Solver screen at step zero

You now have the required blank slate.

Step 4 is to configure Solver options to ensure non-negative values. In addition to the non-negative values we also want to use a quadratic model for estimates and conjugate method for searching optimal solutions.

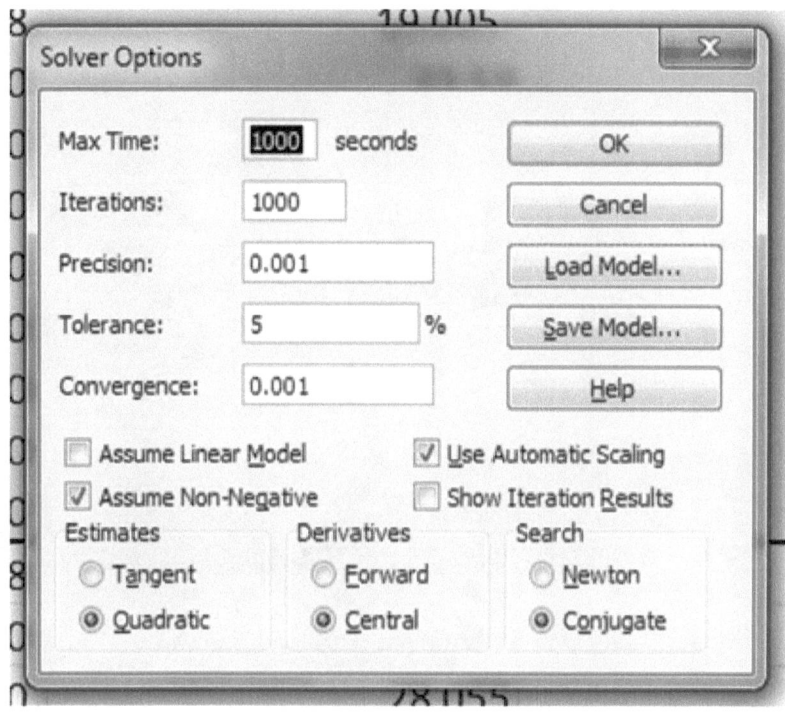

Figure 8 Setting Solver parameters

Step 2 is to setup the objective function cell. This is the Gamma-Vega-Unhedged cell.

Step 3 is to identify the cells Solver will change. This is range of cells under the portfolio allocation weight under the Allocation column.

Once you are done with both steps, the Solver model will look like:

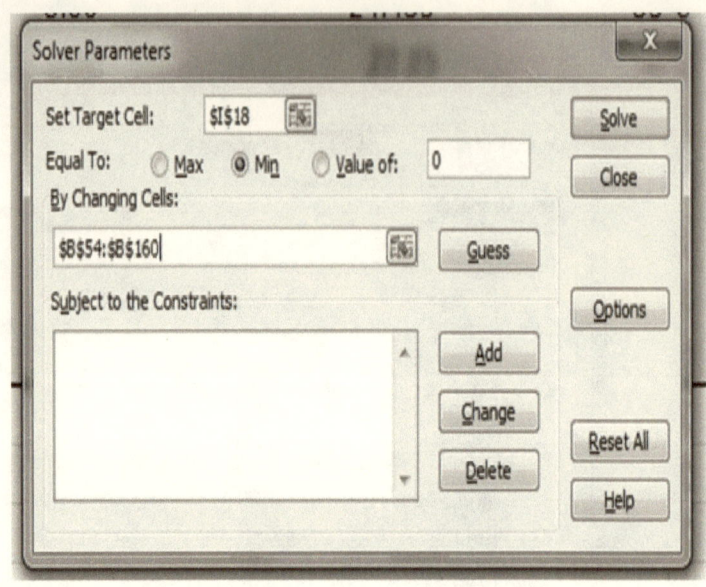

Figure 9 Defining portfolio allocation

Step 4 is to define the constraints with respect to expiry and premium discussed above. Which we do below.

Solver Parameters

Set Target Cell: $G$26

Equal To: ○ Max ◉ Min ○ Value of: 0

By Changing Cells:

$B$54:$B$160

Subject to the Constraints:

$G$23 <= $G$9
$G$25 <= $H$25
$I$18:$I$19 >= 0

Buttons: Solve, Close, Guess, Options, Add, Change, Delete, Reset All, Help

Figure 10 Adding constraints

Here is how the objective function and two of the constraints link up with the relevant cells.

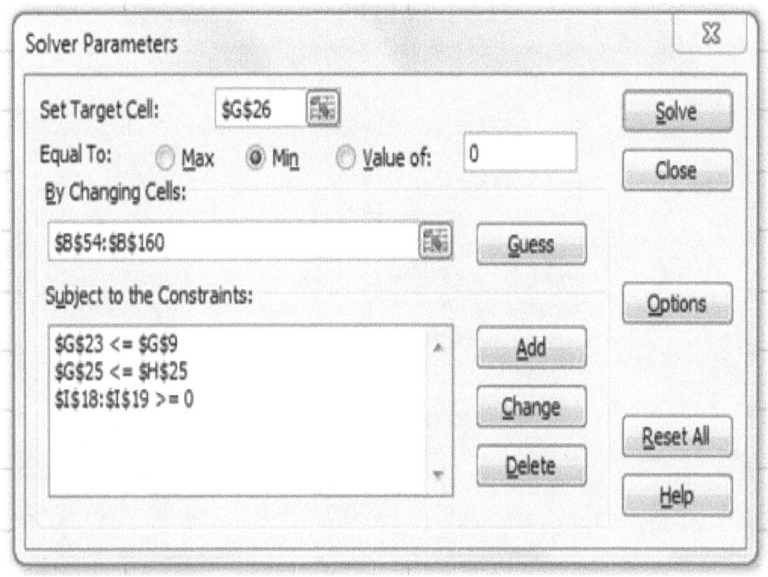

	E	F	G	H	I	J	K	L	M	N
17				Limit	Exposure					
18		Portfolio Gamma	0.01	84%	0.064					
19		Portfolio Vega	0.04	82%	0.205					
20		Portfolio Delta	0.05	91%	0.51					
21		Portfolio Rho	0.01	85%	0.07					
22		Portfolio Theta	0.16	85%	0.91					
23		Portfolio Price	0.17	9%	1.93					
24										
25		Portfolio Expiry	0.299	1	0.70					
26		Gamma-Vega-Unhedged	0.269							
27										

Figure 11 bringing it together

Note that there are a number of additional constraints on the number of option contracts the hedge portfolio can include () as well as the proportion of the original premium available for hedging that we haven't defined. What we would like to do is to try and run this model with these bare minimal conditions and see what kind of a solution Solver throws up and then refine and fine tune the model by adding additional constraints.

If you want to give it a shot, go ahead and press solve to run solver on your newly built Gamma and Vega hedging optimizer model. Before you press Solve make sure that you save your work. What does your solution look like? What is the recommended allocation and cost?

Central clearing

Cleared OTC IRS Swaptions Product Scope

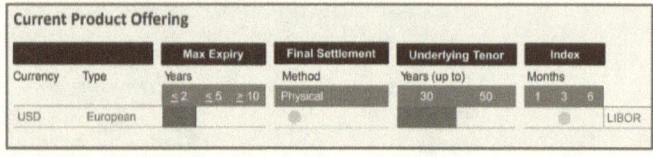

Current Product Offering					
		Max Expiry	**Final Settlement**	**Underlying Tenor**	**Index**
Currency	Type	Years	Method	Years (up to)	Months
		≤2 ≤5 ≥10	Physical	30 50	1 3 6
USD	European				LIBOR

- USD vanilla swaptions
- Includes Straddles, cleared as a single trade or separate payer/receiver
- All enumerations for USD-denominated 3 month LIBOR vanilla interest rate swaps supported, with the exception of:
  - Compounding
  - Forward starting swaps
  - Spreads and stubs

USD Swaptions Product Characteristics

• Straddles, the simultaneous right to pay and receive at the same strike & maturity, are supported & can be cleared as a single trade

• Both upfront and forward premiums are supported

• Premiums may be settled on spot (T+1) through the expiration date +2 of the swaption

• Physical delivery into a cleared CME OTC interest rate swap

transaction

• Effective date equals exercise date +2

• Trade date & cleared date of the underlying swap equals swaption exercise date

• CME performs three validations at the time a trade is submitted to clearing,

same as current workflows

• Account ID must be valid

• Trade must pass credit limits and CME risk filters

• Must meet supported product attributes

• At exercise, the underlying swap transaction bypasses validations (account, credit and

product) & is automatically cleared

Swaption Claim Workflow

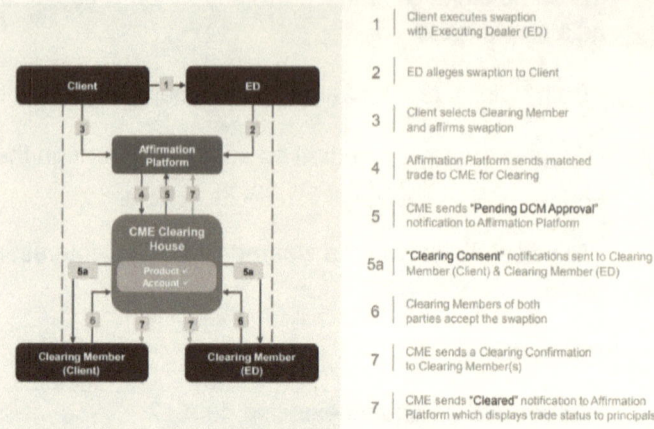

1. Client executes swaption with Executing Dealer (ED)
2. ED alleges swaption to Client
3. Client selects Clearing Member and affirms swaption
4. Affirmation Platform sends matched trade to CME for Clearing
5. CME sends "Pending DCM Approval" notification to Affirmation Platform
5a. "Clearing Consent" notifications sent to Clearing Member (Client) & Clearing Member (ED)
6. Clearing Members of both parties accept the swaption
7. CME sends a Clearing Confirmation to Clearing Member(s)
7. CME sends "Cleared" notification to Affirmation Platform which displays trade status to principals

Margins built to provide 99% coverage over a 5-day closeout period

• Historical scenarios are:

  • Generated using a 5-year look back period

  • Synchronized across all observed tenors

  On the zero curve, across all currencies

  • Scaled using Exponentially Weighted Moving

  Average (EWMA) based volatility forecasts

  • Margin is currently the 99.7th % of portfolio changes (loss) across all scenarios

• The liquidity/concentration model has been enhanced to compute

Liquidity risk at the individual Greek (Delta, Gamma, Vega) and skew Level, then aggregate the sum to determine the portfolio liquidity cost

• Time decay on portfolios is captured to make the model

consistent between swaps and swaptions

Variation Margin =Adjusted NPV (Close) –Adjusted NPV (Previous close)

PAI = -Adjusted NPV (prev bus. day) x Latest Overnight Funding Rate x (Days/360)

Premium (price) of the swaption

FINAL CFTC RULES:
VARIATIONS IN REQUIRED CONDUCT

Base Requirements	Recommendations to any Counterparty
• General prohibition on fraud, manipulation and other abusive practices. • Requirements to "know your counterparty," verify eligibility of counterparties, disclose material information about the swap, and, for certain swaps, to provide a scenario analysis and daily marks. • Requirement to protect confidential counterparty information and comply with fair dealing standards.	• Recommendations trigger a duty by an SD (but not an MSP) to undertake "reasonable diligence" to understand the "risks and rewards" of a swap and to have a "reasonable basis" to believe the swap is "suitable" to the counterparty's needs. • Suitability requirements are met where (i) the counterparty represents it is exercising independent judgment, (ii) the SD represents it is not evaluating the suitability of any recommendation, and (iii) where the SD is "acting as an advisor to a Special Entity," additional requirements are satisfied.

Applicable to All Counterparties { *(bracket spanning the table above)*

Special Entity Requirements	SD is an Advisor to a Special Entity
• A Swap Entity must have a reasonable basis to believe that the Special Entity has a qualified independent representative or a fiduciary under the Employee Retirement Income Security Act of 1979 ("**ERISA**"). • A Swap Entity must disclose to the Special Entity the capacity in which it is acting in connection with the swap, and the differences with other capacities in which it does business with the Special Entity. • An SD (but not an MSP) must comply with "pay-to-play" restrictions with respect to governmental Special Entities.	• An SD (but not an MSP) must act in the "best interests" of the Special Entity and undertake "reasonable efforts" to obtain information necessary to determine that a recommended swap is in the best interests of the Special Entity. • May comply with a safe harbor to avoid advisor status.

Applicable to Special Entity Counterparties { *(bracket spanning the table above)*

The Final CFTC Rules require a Swap Entity to disclose certain information to all non-Swap/SBS Entity counterparties at a "reasonably sufficient" time prior to entering into a swap. The parties may agree on the manner in which the disclosures may be provided, including in a master agreement under which the disclosures are deemed subsequently renewed. 1.

Material Risks.
Swap Entities must disclose the material risks of a swap, which include market, credit, liquidity, foreign currency, legal, operational and any other applicable risks.

    a.   For standardized swaps, standardized risk disclosure in counterparty relationship documentation should be appropriate. For bespoke swaps, more detailed disclosure may be required depending on the complexity of the transaction, the degree and nature of any leverage, the potential for periods of significantly reduced liquidity and the lack of price transparency.

    b.   b. Generally, risk disclosure relates to the risks intrinsic to the contract itself and not the risk of the underlying asset. Yet, where payments or cash-flows are materially affected by the performance of an underlying asset for which there is not publicly available information (e.g., a total return swap on a broad-based index composed of unique assets that the Swap Entity created or acquired), the Final CFTC Rules would require disclosure about the underlier. Note also that disclosure about the Swap Entity's activities in the underlier may be required under the conflicts disclosure requirement discussed below.

Daily Marks.

For swaps cleared by a derivatives clearing organization ("DCO"), a Swap Entity will be required to notify a non-Swap/SBS Entity counterparty of its right to receive the DCO's daily mark. For uncleared swaps, a Swap Entity will be required to provide such counterparty with a daily mark, which would be the mid-market mark of the swap.

Future Outlook

Regulation needed

Many policymakers have strong opinions on the risks of derivatives, but there is no objective economic reason to regulate derivatives as a unique product. To the contrary, it is best to avoid regulating derivatives as a unique product because doing so is bound to result in a complex set of rules filled with special exemptions for select users. Prior to the 2008 financial crisis, derivatives were not regulated as a unique product. Instead, most derivatives—including credit default swaps (CDSs) and other over the counter (OTC) derivatives—were regulated based on who used them and, necessarily, for what purpose. Banks, for instance, were required to account for their derivative exposure within their existing regulatory capital framework, just as they were required to account for loans, repurchase agreements (repos), and other financial risks.

The main problem with the pre-crisis regulatory structure for derivatives and repos was that the bankruptcy code included special exemptions (safe harbors) for derivatives and repos. These safe harbors from core bankruptcy provisions distorted financial markets leading up to the 2008 crisis because they gave derivative and repo users preferred positions relative to other types of creditors. The safe harbors were justified on the grounds that they would prevent systemic financial problems, a theory that proved false in 2008. Nonetheless, the 2010 Dodd–Frank Wall Street Reform and Consumer Protection Act largely ignored these harmful provisions in the bankruptcy code, and implemented a new regulatory framework that regulates OTC derivatives as a unique product. Removing these safe harbors and eliminating the Dodd–Frank framework would improve capital markets by properly incentivizing market participants to account for their financial risks Many commentators have pointed to the enormous *notional* size of the OTC derivatives markets— approximately $700 trillion—as an ominous indicator of the systemic risk that derivatives create.[9] This statistic is misleading for several reasons. To begin, the notional size of the market obscures the fact that derivatives, such as CDSs, improve firms' ability to diversify and reduce their risks. In fact, derivatives securities, such as OTC market CDSs, do not create any new risk. Instead, a CDS merely provides protection to end users by shifting *existing* risks to other firms that are more willing and able to risk their capital. The notional amount of a derivatives contract does not accurately reflect even the amount of capital at risk.

The notional size of an OTC contract merely represents the maximum amount to which a counterparty *could* be exposed, depending on a number of factors.[10] Moreover, firms that sell CDS contracts typically protect their own financial exposure by purchasing separate CDS contracts. JP Morgan, for instance, can buy a CDS contract from Deutsche Bank to protect itself from having to pay on a

CDS it sold to American Airlines. Then, Deutsche Bank can buy a new CDS from Goldman Sachs to protect itself from having to pay JP Morgan, and so on. Thus, while instructive at some level, the notional amount does not accurately reflect either the underlying risk or the amount of that risk to which the counterparties are exposed.

A better measure of the risk that OTC-derivative counterparties take on is the amount of *credit risk* they face. Credit risk, in turn, is the risk that a counterparty may be unable to make the payments to which it agreed in the original contract. The Bank for International Settlements (BIS) estimates total credit risk in the OTC derivatives market with a measure called *gross market value*. The BIS reports that as of December 2015, global OTC derivatives markets contained a gross market value of $14.5 trillion based on a notional amount of $493 trillion.[11] Even this measure, however, fails to account for *netting* among counterparties as well as *collateral*, both of which further reduce counterparties' exposure on derivatives contracts.

The process of netting essentially offsets gains and losses so that OTC counterparties cannot simultaneously default on one contract while accepting payment on another—the *net* difference has to be paid (or received).[12] This practice is standard in the International Swaps and Derivatives Association (ISDA) master agreement, and it binds a defaulting counterparty to offset defaulting (negatively valued) contracts with non-defaulting (positively valued) contracts.[13] Many of the large institutional investors in the OTC derivatives market have multiple contracts with each other, so applying netting to the gross market value in the OTC market reduces aggregate credit exposure even further. In 2013, the ISDA estimated that netting reduced credit exposure in OTC derivatives to less than $4 trillion, a large amount, but far less than $700 trillion.[14] Similarly, the Office of the Comptroller of the Currency (OCC) estimates that U.S. commercial banks and savings associations netted more than 90 percent of their derivatives exposure between 2009 and 2012.[15]

Collateral is property that borrowers provide to lenders as a form of protection in case the borrower fails to pay back what is owed, and derivatives counterparties typically use cash or U.S. Treasury securities for collateral. Counterparties typically post collateral (margin) when they initiate a contract, and also may provide additional collateral (variation margin) as market conditions change. The ISDA estimated that accounting for both netting and collateral reduced the credit exposure in OTC derivatives to $1 trillion in 2013.[16] This figure represents less than 0.5 percent of the notional amount outstanding, and the exposure is roughly consistent with data from both 2011 and 2012 as well.[17] Regulators have to consider all of these issues when developing rules for regulating OTC derivatives.[18]

Pre-Dodd–Frank Regulatory Framework for OTC Derivatives

Prior to the 2010 Dodd–Frank Act, OTC swaps were not separately regulated by either the Commodity Futures Trading Commission (CFTC) or the Securities and Exchange Commission (SEC), but the overwhelming majority of these swaps were regulated by state and federal banking regulators.[19]Historically, large banks have always been the heaviest users of interest-rate swaps, the type of swap that accounts for more than 80 percent of the OTC derivatives market. Thus for the bulk of the OTC derivatives market, it is completely false to say that OTC derivatives were unregulated. Federal banking regulators, including the Federal Reserve and the OCC, constantly monitor banks' financial condition, especially the banks' swaps exposure.[20]

The main method that banking regulators used to regulate banks' swap exposure was to ensure that banks accounted for OTC derivatives when calculating their regulatory capital. Even the very first iteration of the Basel capital requirements, which were implemented in the late 1980s, required banks to account for their swaps when calculating capital ratios. In particular, banks had to hold capital against the *credit-risk equivalent* to their swaps, a method that essentially treated derivatives as a type of loan in banks' risk-adjusted assets.[21] Simply put, none of these derivatives transactions took place outside bank regulators' purview, and there is no shortage of public acknowledgements attesting to this fact. For instance, a 1993 Boston Federal Reserve paper notes that "[b]ank regulators have recognized the credit risk of swaps and instituted capital requirements for them and for other off-balance-sheet activities, as part of the new risk-based capital requirements for banks."[22]

As a result, OTC derivatives were not regulated as a specific product in the way that, for example, gasoline is regulated. Instead, OTC derivatives were regulated on the basis of who used them and, necessarily, for what purpose. If, for example, American Airlines negotiated an OTC derivative contract with Wells Fargo, federal banking regulations would require Wells Fargo to account for that contract within its normal regulatory capital framework. In other words, Wells Fargo was required to account for its OTC derivatives exposure within the same framework it was required to account for loans and other financial risks. Although American Airlines was not regulated by banking regulators, the company had to disclose the financial risks associated with its derivatives contracts based on standards adopted by the Financial Accounting Standards Board (FASB).[23]

Ideally, the regulatory framework for derivatives would focus exclusively on fostering accurate disclosure of relevant information, even by financial companies.[24] However, given that banks—not commercial companies, such as American Airlines—in the pre-Dodd–Frank era were regulated with a risk-based capital framework, the older approach made perfect sense. Then, as now, there was nothing particularly unique about OTC derivatives requiring special product-based regulations for all users. Indeed, it is best to avoid regulating OTC derivatives as a unique product because that type of regulation invites rules that favor certain users over others. Nonetheless, the Dodd–Frank Act imposed product-based regulations on much of the OTC derivatives market.

Title VII of Dodd–Frank imposes a requirement to clear more OTC derivatives through central counterparties (CCPs), and also gives the CFTC and the SEC explicit authority to regulate the OTC swaps markets and market participants.[25] Many commercial users of derivatives have exemptions from the new rules, but banking regulators remain responsible for certifying that banks are meeting their regulatory capital ratios when they use OTC swaps. Title VII did virtually nothing to fix the problems that contributed to the 2008 financial crisis, and the new rules—particularly the clearing mandate—have likely further concentrated financial risks in U.S. markets.

The Dodd–Frank framework is also harmful because it ignores particularly damaging derivatives exemptions in the bankruptcy code. In fact, Dodd–Frank ignores similarly risky bankruptcy provisions for repos.[26] Both derivatives and repos, a type of short-term loan secured with collateral, share special bankruptcy provisions that favor their users relative to other creditors.[27] This special treatment contributed to major market distortions leading up to the 2008 financial crisis because it gave repo and derivatives counterparties preferred positions over other creditors.

Overview of Key Provisions in Bankruptcy

Dodd–Frank took a misguided approach to actively regulating OTC derivatives and, perhaps worse, failed to address special bankruptcy provisions that favor OTC derivative and repo users relative to ordinary creditors. The current bankruptcy code was enacted in 1978, and Congress has steadily expanded safe harbors for derivatives and repos, as well as other financial contracts.[28] A brief overview of the bankruptcy process highlights how this special treatment can distort financial markets by favoring certain counterparties over other creditors.[29]

A firm (the debtor) typically files for bankruptcy protection under Chapter 11 of the U.S. Code, meaning that it seeks protection from creditors who may seek control of the firm's assets because they fear nonpayment. A main goal of this protection is to enable the debtor to remain in business and pay its creditors what they are owed over time. When a Chapter 11 bankruptcy filing begins, the court creates an "estate" that consists of virtually all of the debtor's assets as of the petition date.[30] To ensure that the estate remains a viable business, the bankruptcy filing triggers a provision known as the *automatic stay*, a kind of financial time-out.[31]

The stay remains in effect until a bankruptcy judge—sort of a referee in the process—says otherwise, at which time the debtor and the creditors begin a coordinated effort to resolve the debtor's financial situation equitably across similar creditors. In general, the bankruptcy filing strips creditors of many contractual rights they would normally have. For instance, when the debtor files bankruptcy, the stay immediately and automatically prohibits creditors from suing the debtor, or taking any other action to collect what they are owed. The stay even prohibits secured creditors from selling or seizing the collateral (cash or securities) they hold. This process is meant to protect the debtor from a mad rush of creditors trying to obtain what they are owed before anyone else.

The bankruptcy code provides several other protections to help ensure that similarly situated creditors are treated in an equitable manner (meaning that they share any losses in an equitable manner). For example, creditors generally have to seek the court's permission to *set off* what they owe the debtor against any amounts the debtor may owe them.[32] Additionally, the debtor (or a court-appointed trustee) can generally force creditors to return any *preferential transfers*.[33] For instance, a creditor may have to return a payment made within 90 days of bankruptcy if that payment would have made the creditor better off than had the transfer not been made. The amount would have to be returned to the estate so that it would improve the collective position of the creditors.

Similarly, the debtor generally has the power to avoid fraudulent conveyances.[34] For instance, sales or transfers of assets at less than fair value within two years of the filing date can be reversed to benefit *all*creditors. More broadly, creditors generally cannot terminate their contracts with the debtor simply because the firm filed for bankruptcy protection. In fact, even if a contract includes a clause that makes the debtor's bankruptcy a default (an *ipso facto* clause) the clause is generally not enforceable.[35]However, debtors can generally choose which uncompleted contracts (those which have elements of both assets and liabilities for the estate) to reject.[36]

Distortions arise because the bankruptcy code provides derivatives and repo users with safe harbors that leave them in a preferred position relative to ordinary creditors. Based on what occurred during the 2008 financial crisis (discussed below), these safe harbors have at least partially defeated the main purpose of bankruptcy protection. In particular, these safe harbors prevented firms from using the bankruptcy code to reorganize and continue operating because they encouraged certain creditors to individually seek payments outside a collective bankruptcy proceeding rather than negotiate with debtors inside bankruptcy.[37]

Safe Harbors for Derivatives and Repos

The 2005 Bankruptcy Abuse Prevention and Consumer Protection Act expanded several key safe harbors largely by defining the term *swap agreement* to include effectively all derivatives contracts.[38] In particular, this change extended safe harbors to virtually all derivatives users such that the entire market was exempt from the automatic stay and preference provisions. The 2005 act also expanded the definition of *repurchase agreement* to include "mortgage related securities...mortgage loans, interests in mortgage related securities or mortgage loans," as well as several additional items.[39] Thus, since 2005, the bankruptcy code exempted derivatives and repos from two core provisions of bankruptcy: the automatic stay and preference protections.[40]

The code also exempts these contracts from bankruptcy's anti–*ipso facto*rules, the trustee's power to avoid fraudulent conveyances,[41] and even from limitations on a non-debtor's ability to set off obligations owed to the debtor. Unlike ordinary creditors, derivatives counterparties can automatically terminate their contracts as soon as a debtor files for bankruptcy protection.[42] The fact that the debtor's counterparties can seize collateral free from preference protections was a feature that proved especially harmful during the 2008 crisis. Collectively, these safe harbors mean that all derivatives and repo users are—as they were prior to the 2008 crisis—protected parties relative to ordinary creditors.

Weak Justification for Safe Harbors. These safe harbors have been justified on various grounds, most of which relate in some way to systemic crises.[43]For instance, in the early 1980s, industry advocates argued that derivatives markets were too complex to treat counterparties like other creditors, and that if safe harbors were not provided "the whole system would become paralyzed" in a bankruptcy.[44] Similarly, in 1983, Fed Chair Paul Volcker suggested a safe harbor was necessary to protect the repo market given that repos were a main tool of monetary policy. Volcker also argued that limiting these special protections to repo transactions of $1 million or more would suffice, thus avoiding the need to provide broad exceptions to existing bankruptcy laws.[45]

A common argument for safe harbors is that subjecting derivatives counterparties to the automatic stay could cause multiple firms to fail, thus leading to a financial crisis, a recession, or both. A bankruptcy filing could, for instance, cause the firm's counterparties to "run," quickly closing out their positions and selling collateral to avoid being subjected to an automatic stay. This run could result in rapidly declining asset prices, thus destabilizing financial markets. Similarly, proponents of these special exemptions argue that safe harbors allow counterparties to quickly cancel contracts and enter new hedges (with other counterparties), thus ensuring their financial health and avoiding financial market distress.[46]

Aside from whether safe harbors can actually mitigate systemic risk, systemic concerns do not justify blanket exemptions from core bankruptcy provisions. By definition, systemic risk concerns could only justify, at most, exemptions for the largest or most systemically important derivatives counterparties. Identifying such institutions—even using broad guidelines such as those in Dodd–Frank—is far from an objective exercise, a problem which highlights that such safe harbors necessarily provide preferential treatment to certain creditors over others. For this reason alone, providing these safe harbors requires an overwhelmingly compelling justification. This justification simply does not exist, and the 2008 financial crisis provides evidence that safe harbors worsen, rather than mitigate, systemic risk.

Safe Harbors Increase Risk of Financial Turmoil. The 2008 crisis showed that most of these arguments for giving special exemptions to derivatives counterparties are deeply flawed. First, the notion that the automatic stay safe harbor would prevent a run proved to be incorrect. Bear Stearns's counterparties ran before Bear was even considering bankruptcy.[47]Lehman Brothers's problems were also exacerbated by safe harbors. Immediately before the firm collapsed, JP Morgan seized $17 billion in securities and cash (Lehman's collateral) and demanded an additional $5 billion payment.[48] Lehman effectively had no choice but to come up with the additional collateral, thus worsening its liquidity position.

Lehman could not file bankruptcy to prevent Morgan from selling the collateral because of the safe harbors, and Lehman had no reason to expect that it could retrieve the payment as a special preference if it did file for bankruptcy. Furthermore, the lead attorney in the Lehman bankruptcy case testified to Congress that the lack of an automatic stay contributed to confusion at the outset of the filing.[49] The safe harbors also encouraged Lehman's accounting manipulation known as Repo 105, an end-of-quarter transaction used to disguise the company's true leverage. Had repos been treated as secure loans without the safe harbors—as the economic structure of a repo actually justifies—it is unlikely that Lehman could have conducted the Repo 105 transaction.[50]

The safe harbors also played a negative role in the near failure of American International Group (AIG).[51] The company's counterparties increasingly demanded additional collateral for its large CDS portfolio, thus threatening to bankrupt the company. As with Lehman, AIG would have been able to refuse the collateral demands and expect protection had there been no safe harbors for the CDSs.[52] Even if the safe harbors only partly contributed to the runs on these counterparties, it is clear that the safe harbors did not prevent the type of systemic problems that advocates suggested they would.

Aside from the added incentive to run, the safe harbors likely induced firms to rely more heavily on derivatives and repos than they would have in absence of the special protections. For instance, Bear Stearns's liabilities consisted of only 7 percent repos in 1990, but by 2008 they consisted of 25 percent repos.[53] Data also show that the portion of *total investment bank*assets financed by repos doubled between 2000 and 2007.[54] Whether the growing market led to legislative action to further support the market, or whether the legislative amendments to the bankruptcy code led to the growing market is irrelevant. Either way, the market would not have supported such high increases in leverage without the special protections, which is precisely why the safe harbors should not be provided.

The safe harbors also lead to more subtle adverse effects, such as diminishing the incentive to monitor counterparties and to prepare (or even file) for bankruptcy.[55] It is certainly true that eliminating these safe harbors may cause firms to rely less on these short-term debt instruments, and to price in higher risks than they do currently. However, this outcome is not a market failure: It is precisely how markets function when the participants have the proper incentives to monitor their risks.

The fact that the Federal Deposit Insurance Corporation (FDIC) has for decades implemented a special failure-resolution process for banks that imposes a one-day stay on a bank's derivative and repo counterparties makes the case for economy-wide safe harbors even less compelling.[56]This temporary stay for banks provides additional evidence that the safe harbors exacerbated the 2008 crisis because markets froze in the *nonbanking* sector where there were safe harbors, not in the banking sector where a temporary stay was in effect. Rather than relying on contracting and special rules to prevent excessive financial risks, Congress should enact reforms that expose financial market participants to more market discipline.

Shifted SABR

The shifted SABR is the first and simplest extension of the SABR model to the low-interest-rate environment. Despite several short comings it is widely used by practitioners. It inherits the advantages and intuitive parameters of the SABR model. Under the shifted SABR the forward rate has the following dynamics:

$$dF_t = \sigma_t (F_t + s)^\beta dW_t^1, \quad F(0) = f$$
$$d\sigma_t = \nu \sigma_t dW_t^2, \quad \sigma(0) = \alpha$$

where $dW_t^1 dW_t^2 = \rho dt$ and s a positive deterministic shift.

The shift changes the lower boundary from 0 to −s, thereby allowing Ft to reach negative levels. The shift can be either calibrated as an additional parameter of the SABR model or fixed prior to calibration, the first option is not adapted as calibrating the shift only influences the

skew (already controlled by β) without adding a new degree of freedom

This example shows how to price swaption with negative strikes by using the Shifted SABR model. The market Shifted Black volatilities are used to calibrate the Shifted SABR model parameters. The calibrated Shifted SABR model is then used to compute the Shifted Black volatilities for negative strikes.

The swaptions with negative strikes are then priced using the computed Shifted Black volatilities and the swaptionbyblk function with the 'Shift' parameter set to the prespecified shift. Similarly, Shifted SABR Greeks can be computed by using the optsensbysabr function by setting the 'Shift' parameter. Finally, from the swaption prices, the probability density of the underlying asset is computed to show that the swaption prices imply positive probability densities for some negative strikes.

```
ValuationDate = '5-Apr-2016';
EndDates = datemnth(ValuationDate,[1 2 3 6 9 12*[1 2 3 4
5 6 7 8 9 10 12]])';
ZeroRates = [-0.34 -0.29 -0.25 -0.13 -0.07 -0.02 0.010
0.025 ...
    0.031 0.040 0.052 0.090 0.190 0.290 0.410 0.520]'/100;
Compounding = 1;
RateSpec =
intenvset('ValuationDate',ValuationDate,'StartDates',Valuat
ionDate, ...
'EndDates',EndDates,'Rates',ZeroRates,'Compounding',C
ompounding)
```

```
RateSpec = struct with fields:
        FinObj: 'RateSpec'
   Compounding: 1
          Disc: [16x1 double]
         Rates: [16x1 double]
      EndTimes: [16x1 double]
    StartTimes: [16x1 double]
      EndDates: [16x1 double]
    StartDates: 736425
 ValuationDate: 736425
```

```
Basis: 0
EndMonthRule: 1
```

```
SwaptionSettle = '5-Apr-2016';
SwaptionExerciseDate = '5-Apr-2017';
SwapMaturity = '5-Apr-2022';
Reset = 1;
OptSpec = 'call';
TimeToExercise =
yearfrac(SwaptionSettle,SwaptionExerciseDate)
```

se **swapbyzero** to compute the forward swap rate.

```
LegRate = [NaN 0];  % To compute the forward swap rate,
set the fixed rate to NaN.
[~, CurrentForwardValue] =
swapbyzero(RateSpec,LegRate,SwaptionSettle,SwapMatu
rity,...
'StartDate',SwaptionExerciseDate)
```

Specify amount of shift in decimals for Shifted Black and
Shifted SABR models.

```
Shift = 0.008;  % 0.8 percent shift
```

```
MarketShiftedBlackVolatilities = [21.1; 15.3; 14.0; 14.6;
16.0; 17.7; 19.8; 23.9; 26.2]/100;
StrikeGrid = [-0.5; -0.25; -0.125; 0; 0.125; 0.25; 0.5; 1.0;
1.5]/100;
MarketStrikes = CurrentForwardValue + StrikeGrid;
ATMShiftedBlackVolatility =
MarketShiftedBlackVolatilities(StrikeGrid==0);
```

This function solves the Shifted SABR at-the-money
volatility equation as a polynomial of Alpha. Note the
addition of Shift to CurrentForwardValue.

```
alpharoots = @(Rho,Nu) roots([...
    (1 - Beta)^2*TimeToExercise/24/(CurrentForwardValue
+ Shift)^(2 - 2*Beta) ...
```

```
    Rho*Beta*Nu*TimeToExercise/4/(CurrentForwardValue
+ Shift)^(1 - Beta) ...
    (1 + (2 - 3*Rho^2)*Nu^2*TimeToExercise/24) ...
    -ATMShiftedBlackVolatility*(CurrentForwardValue +
Shift)^(1 - Beta)]);
```

This function converts at-the-money volatility into Alpha by picking the smallest positive real root.

```
atmVol2ShiftedSabrAlpha = @(Rho,Nu)
min(real(arrayfun(@(x) ...
    x*(x>0) + realmax*(x<0 || abs(imag(x))>1e-6),
alpharoots(Rho,Nu))));
```

```
objFun = @(X) MarketShiftedBlackVolatilities - ...
    blackvolbysabr(atmVol2ShiftedSabrAlpha(X(1), X(2)), ...
    Beta, X(1), X(2), SwaptionSettle,
SwaptionExerciseDate, CurrentForwardValue, ...
    MarketStrikes, 'Shift', Shift);
```

```
options = optimoptions('lsqnonlin','Display','none');
X = lsqnonlin(objFun, [0 0.5], [-1 0], [1 Inf], options);
Rho = X(1);
Nu = X(2);
```

Get the final Alpha from the calibrated parameters.

```
Alpha = atmVol2ShiftedSabrAlpha(Rho, Nu)
```

```
Alpha = 0.0133
```
Show the calibrated Shifted SABR parameters.

```
CalibratedPrameters = array2table([Shift Alpha Beta Rho
Nu],...
    'VariableNames',{'Shift' 'Alpha' 'Beta' 'Rho' 'Nu'},...
    'RowNames',{'1Y into 5Y'})
```

Calibrated Prameters=1×5					
	Shift	Alpha	Beta	Rho	Nu
1Y into 5Y	0.008	0.013345	0.5	0.46698	0.49816

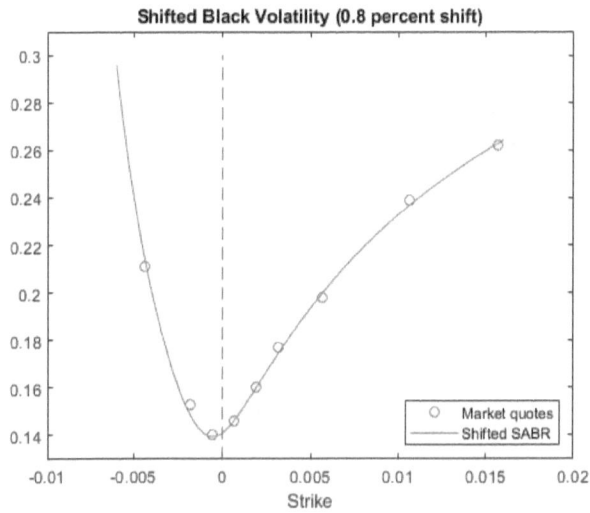

```
SwaptionPrices = swaptionbyblk(RateSpec, OptSpec,
Strikes, SwaptionSettle, SwaptionExerciseDate, ...
   SwapMaturity, SABRShiftedBlackVolatilities, 'Reset',
Reset, 'Shift', Shift);
figure;
plot(Strikes, SwaptionPrices, 'r');
h = gca;
line([0,0],[min(h.YLim),max(h.YLim)],'LineStyle','--');
xlabel('Strike');
title ('Swaption Price');
```

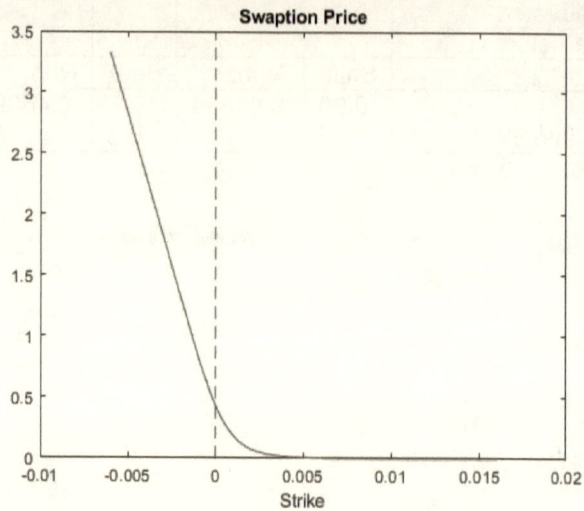

```
ShiftedSABRDelta = optsensbysabr(RateSpec, Alpha,
Beta, Rho, Nu, SwaptionSettle, ...
SwaptionExerciseDate, CurrentForwardValue, Strikes,
OptSpec, 'Shift', Shift);

figure;
plot(Strikes,ShiftedSABRDelta,'r-');
ylim([-0.002 1.002]);
h = gca;
line([0,0],[min(h.YLim),max(h.YLim)],'LineStyle','--');
xlabel('Strike');
title ('Delta');
```

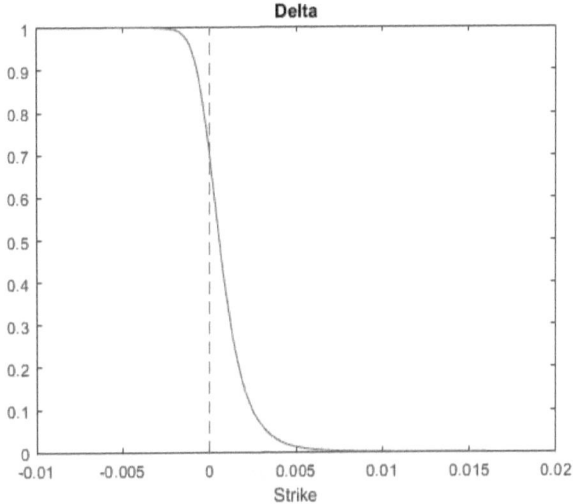

Delta

How Regulators Should Account for OTC Derivatives

There is no objective economic reason to treat derivatives users preferentially relative to any other set of creditors in a bankruptcy case. Thus, a key component of reforming the regulatory framework for derivatives and repos is to remove their bankruptcy safe harbors. Some scholars have argued for a more cautious approach, such as implementing an automatic stay that lasts for 48 hours or 72 hours, and recent bankruptcy-reform legislation includes a 48-hour automatic stay for derivatives and repos that would apply to counterparties of certain large financial institutions.[57]

Similarly, some have argued that *most* of the safe harbors should be eliminated, but that an automatic-stay safe harbor should remain in place for *cash-like* collateral used in repo transactions.[58] This type of proposal is justified on the grounds that repo markets are volatile and their values can change dramatically over very short time periods, with counterparties constantly recalibrating margin and collateral requirements. Economically, though, these market attributes alone provide no justification for bankruptcy safe harbors—they merely describe factors that counterparties would price differently were there no safe harbors.[59] In other words, removing all of the safe harbors would all but certainly impact the market because counterparties would have to account for more risk, an outcome which should be applauded.

There is also no objective economic reason to regulate derivatives as a unique product. The Dodd–Frank Act took such an approach, and imposed product-based regulations on much of the OTC derivatives market. The outcome of these Dodd–Frank changes is more highly concentrated financial risks, and an incredibly complex set of rules filled with special exemptions and safe harbors. This is exactly the wrong approach because it creates a framework that invites special-interest lobbying for rules that favor certain market participants over others. Ideally, the regulatory framework should provide no special protections for derivative or repo counterparties and focus exclusively on fostering accurate disclosure of relevant information. In an optimal regulatory framework, this disclosure focus could even be applied to banking institutions.

Though the current framework is far from ideal, bringing more market discipline and less taxpayer backing to the banking industry would lessen the need for statutory capital requirements and complex derivatives rules. Even outside that ideal framework, there are many ways that regulatory capital rules for derivatives can be simplified, thus moving toward greater reliance on disclosure. For instance, regulatory relief could be provided to banks that choose to meet a higher capital requirement that accounts for derivatives exposure in a straightforward, transparent manner. This type of leverage ratio (referred to as a regulatory off-ramp) could, for example, include net credit exposure from derivatives and a flat percentage of notional derivative contracts in a bank's total assets.[60] Accounting for derivatives exposure in this type of straightforward, transparent manner would introduce much-needed market discipline to banks and derivatives counterparties.

Congress should implement the following changes to move the U.S. regulatory framework for derivatives toward an ideal system:

- **Repeal Title VII of Dodd–Frank.** Title VII of Dodd–Frank imposes a requirement to clear more OTC derivatives through central counterparties (CCPs), and also gives the CFTC and the SEC explicit authority to regulate the OTC swaps markets and market participants. Title VII is based on the false notion that a lack of regulation caused the financial crisis, and it has served mainly to centralize risk in a small number of large firms, increase moral hazard, and increase the likelihood of a future financial crisis. Repealing Title VII largely reverts to a framework where derivatives are regulated based on which market participants use them and for which purpose, rather than regulated as a unique product. Banks, for instance, would not be able to use derivatives or repos outside their regulatory capital framework if Title VII is repealed.

- **Simplify derivatives regulation for banks.** Banks are regulated differently than most companies largely because taxpayers back FDIC deposit insurance and loan guarantees, as well as (ultimately) Federal Reserve emergency lending. These forms of taxpayer support have to be removed in order for the U.S. framework to fully utilize market-based regulations that rely mainly on disclosure. In the meantime, Congress can provide regulatory off-ramps to banks that elect to meet higher, simpler capital standards, similar to the approach taken in the Financial CHOICE Act. While many other reforms are needed to bring more market discipline to bear on banks and derivatives counterparties, accounting for banks' derivatives exposure in a straightforward, transparent manner (in a regulatory off-ramp requirement) would partly accomplish this goal.

Any off-ramp leverage ratio could, for example, include net credit exposure and a flat percentage of notional derivative contracts (both commonly reported already) in total assets. Such a reform would eventually lower the reliance on complex, opaque rules that favor those banks most heavily involved in derivatives markets.

- **Remove safe harbors for repos and derivatives.** The bankruptcy code should be amended so that repo and derivatives counterparties no longer have safe harbors that position them as preferred creditors. Specifically, safe harbors from the automatic stay, anti–*ipso facto* rules, and preference and fraudulent conveyances rules should all be eliminated. A temporary automatic stay (for all derivatives and repos) of 48 hours to 72 hours is a good intermediate step, but any such temporary stay should automatically sunset after several years so that the safe harbor is completely eliminated. These safe harbors should be removed for CCPs as well. Even if systemic risk concerns were valid, they would not justify blanket exemptions from core bankruptcy provisions. By definition, systemic risk concerns could only justify, at most, exemptions for the largest or most systemically important derivatives counterparties. Providing safe harbors in this manner would blatantly provide special financial protection to a small group of financial firms. Regardless, safe harbors actually worsened credit market turmoil during the 2008 crisis, while safe harbor advocates had claimed the special exemptions would avoid such problems.

Conclusion

There is nothing particularly unique about derivatives that would require them to have special product-based regulations. Indeed, it is best to avoid regulating derivatives as a unique product because that type of regulation invites rules that favor certain users over others. Ideally, the regulatory framework for derivatives would focus exclusively on fostering accurate disclosure of relevant information, even by financial companies. The U.S. regulatory framework has gone in exactly the wrong direction for decades, providing special exemptions to an increasingly complex set of rules and, as of 2010, regulating derivatives as specific products. Derivatives themselves should no longer be regulated as a distinct product, and the changes implemented by Title VII of the 2010 Dodd–Frank Act should be repealed.

Another main problem with the existing framework—which Dodd–Frank barely addressed—is that the bankruptcy code provides derivatives and repo users with exemptions that leave them in a preferred position relative to ordinary creditors. The turmoil in financial markets during the 2008 crisis shows that the main arguments for giving safe harbors to derivatives and repo counterparties are deeply flawed. Rather than mitigate systemic risk, the safe harbors increased reliance on derivatives and repos, provided higher incentives to run on counterparties, and decreased the incentive to monitor counterparties, as well as to prepare (or even file) for bankruptcy. All such safe harbors should be removed from the bankruptcy code to eliminate disparate treatment for similarly situated creditors.

—*Norbert J. Michel, PhD, is a Research Fellow in Financial Regulations in the Thomas A. Roe Institute for Economic Policy Studies, of the Institute for Economic Freedom and Opportunity, at The Heritage Foundation.*

This report is part of *Prosperity Unleashed: Smarter Financial Regulation*. Government policies have—for decades—empowered regulators to manage private risks and mitigate private losses in an effort to prevent financial-sector turmoil from spreading to the rest of the economy. This approach, rarely contemplated in nonfinancial industries, has demonstrably failed. *Prosperity Unleashed: Smarter Financial Regulation* provides solutions to the core regulatory problems that existed in U.S. financial markets long before the 2008 financial crisis.

Appendix

The following, quoted, text compares the legal definitions of *repurchase agreement* and *swap agreement* before and after the 2005 Bankruptcy Abuse Prevention and Consumer Protection Act was enacted.

Repurchase Agreement as defined in U.S. Code prior to the Bankruptcy Abuse Prevention and Consumer Protection Act of 2005.[61]

"repurchase agreement" (which definition also applies to a reverse repurchase agreement) means an agreement, including related terms, which provides for the transfer of certificates of deposit, eligible bankers' acceptances, or securities that are direct obligations of, or that are fully guaranteed as to principal and interest by, the United States or any agency of the United States against the transfer of funds by the transferee of such certificates of deposit, eligible bankers' acceptances, or securities with a simultaneous agreement by such transferee to transfer to the transferor thereof certificates of deposit, eligible bankers' acceptances, or securities as described above, at a date certain not later than one year after such transfers or on demand, against the transfer of funds.

Repurchase Agreement as defined in U.S. Code after the Bankruptcy Abuse Prevention and Consumer Protection Act of 2005.[62]

The term "repurchase agreement" (which definition also applies to a reverse repurchase agreement)—(A) means—

(i) an agreement, including related terms, which provides for the transfer of one or more certificates of deposit, mortgage related securities (as defined in section 3 of the

Securities Exchange Act of 1934), mortgage loans, interests in mortgage related securities or mortgage loans, eligible bankers' acceptances, qualified foreign government securities (defined as a security that is a direct obligation of, or that is fully guaranteed by, the central government of a member of the Organization for Economic Cooperation and Development), or securities that are direct obligations of, or that are fully guaranteed by, the United States or any agency of the United States against the transfer of funds by the transferee of such certificates of deposit, eligible bankers' acceptances, securities, mortgage loans, or interests, with a simultaneous agreement by such transferee to transfer to the transferor thereof certificates of deposit, eligible bankers' acceptance, securities, mortgage loans, or interests of the kind described in this clause, at a date certain not later than 1 year after such transfer or on demand, against the transfer of funds;

(ii) any combination of agreements or transactions referred to in clauses (i) and (iii);

(iii) an option to enter into an agreement or transaction referred to in clause (i) or (ii);

(iv) a master agreement that provides for an agreement or transaction referred to in clause (i), (ii), or (iii), together with all supplements to any such master agreement, without regard to whether such master agreement provides for an agreement or transaction that is not a repurchase agreement under this paragraph, except that such master agreement shall be considered to be a repurchase agreement under this paragraph only with respect to each agreement or transaction under the master agreement that is referred to in clause (i), (ii), or (iii); or

(v) any security agreement or arrangement or other credit enhancement related to any agreement or transaction referred to in clause (i), (ii), (iii), or (iv), including any guarantee or reimbursement obligation by or to a repo participant or financial participant in connection with any agreement or transaction referred to in any such clause, but not to exceed the damages in connection with any such agreement or transaction, measured in accordance with section 562 of this title; and (B) does not include a repurchase obligation under a participation in a commercial mortgage loan.

Swap Agreement as defined in U.S. Code prior to the Bankruptcy Abuse Prevention and Consumer Protection Act of 2005.[63]

"swap agreement" means—

(A) an agreement (including terms and conditions incorporated by reference therein) which is a rate swap agreement, basis swap, forward rate agreement, commodity swap, interest rate option, forward foreign exchange agreement, spot foreign exchange agreement, rate cap agreement, rate floor agreement, rate collar agreement, currency swap agreement, cross-currency rate swap agreement, currency option, any other similar agreement (including any option to enter into any of the foregoing);

(B) any combination of the foregoing; or

(C) a master agreement for any of the foregoing together with all supplements.

Swap Agreement as defined in U.S. Code after the Bankruptcy Abuse Prevention and Consumer Protection Act of 2005.[64]

The term "swap agreement"—

(A) means—

(i) any agreement, including the terms and conditions incorporated by reference in such agreement, which is—

(I) an interest rate swap, option, future, or forward agreement, including a rate floor, rate cap, rate collar, cross-currency rate swap, and basis swap;

(II) a spot, same day-tomorrow, tomorrow-next, forward, or other foreign exchange, precious metals, or other commodity agreement;

(III) a currency swap, option, future, or forward agreement;

(IV) an equity index or equity swap, option, future, or forward agreement;

(V) a debt index or debt swap, option, future, or forward agreement;

(VI) a total return, credit spread or credit swap, option, future, or forward agreement;

(VII) a commodity index or a commodity swap, option, future, or forward agreement;

(VIII) a weather swap, option, future, or forward agreement;

(IX) an emissions swap, option, future, or forward agreement; or

(X) an inflation swap, option, future, or forward agreement;

(ii) any agreement or transaction that is similar to any other agreement or transaction referred to in this paragraph and that—

(I) is of a type that has been, is presently, or in the future becomes, the subject of recurrent dealings in the swap or other derivatives markets (including terms and conditions incorporated by reference therein); and

(II) is a forward, swap, future, option, or spot transaction on one or more rates, currencies, commodities, equity securities, or other equity instruments, debt securities or other debt instruments, quantitative measures associated with an occurrence, extent of an occurrence, or contingency associated with a financial, commercial, or economic consequence, or economic or financial indices or measures of economic or financial risk or value;

(iii) any combination of agreements or transactions referred to in this subparagraph;

(iv) any option to enter into an agreement or transaction referred to in this subparagraph;

(v) a master agreement that provides for an agreement or transaction referred to in clause (i), (ii), (iii), or (iv), together with all supplements to any such master agreement, and without regard to whether the master agreement contains an agreement or transaction that is not a swap agreement under this paragraph, except that the master agreement shall be considered to be a swap agreement under this paragraph only with respect to each agreement or transaction under the master agreement that is referred to in clause (i), (ii), (iii), or (iv); or

(vi) any security agreement or arrangement or other credit enhancement related to any agreements or transactions referred to in clause (i) through (v), including any guarantee or reimbursement obligation by or to a swap participant or financial participant in connection with any agreement or transaction referred to in any such clause, but not to exceed the damages in connection with any such agreement or transaction, measured in accordance with section 562; and

(B) is applicable for purposes of this title only, and shall not be construed or applied so as to challenge or affect the characterization, definition, or treatment of any swap agreement under any other statute, regulation, or rule, including the Gramm–Leach–Bliley Act, the Legal Certainty for Bank Products Act of 2000, the securities laws (as such term is defined in section 3(a)(47) of the Securities Exchange Act of 1934) and the Commodity Exchange Act.53B)

Regulatory Disruption
The interplay of regulatory trends and strategic priorities

Persuaded that lax regulation of financial derivatives contributed to the 2008 financial crisis, policymakers in Congress and the Obama Administration have adopted a knee-jerk solution: regulate everything.

The Obama Administration has proposed and the House Financial Services and Senate Banking Committees have each approved schemes for regulating derivatives that differ in many details. But the proposals agree on the most significant point: that derivatives regulation must be "comprehensive." By "comprehensive," regulators mean that every financial product, every buyer, every seller, every intermediary, and every transaction must be regulated unless expressly exempted by statute or decree.

The premise supporting the blanket regulatory diktat—that every derivative contract poses systemic risk to the financial system—is unproven, the application overly broad, and the resulting bureaucratic burden excessively heavy.

- Resist simplistic calls for "more regulation" until proponents demonstrate that particular types of derivatives caused or intensified the financial crisis;

- Apply any new regulation to the derivative products, institutions, or market mechanisms that caused economic harm; and
- Tailor regulation to address specific problems or harms identified.

Are All Derivatives the Same?

Derivatives are financial instruments used to transfer risk from a party seeking to "hedge" (limit) risk to a party willing—for a fee—to assume the risk. Risks transferred may be related to prices (whether they rise, fall, or fluctuate), interest rates, exchange rates, or they may be related to whether a third party will pay its debts.

Derivatives play a productive economic role by allowing firms to plan based on stable economic factors while transferring the risk (including the potential reward) of economic disruptions to others who are willing and able to assume it. The term *derivative* applies to this diverse set of products because their value is determined by reference to another underlying product or transaction.

Some derivatives, such as commodity or stock futures, are regulated by the CFTC or SEC. Other derivatives related to interest rates, foreign exchange, and debt (called "financial derivatives") are traded largely OTC among banks, whose operations are regulated by the Federal Reserve and other banking agencies.

Financial derivatives differ significantly from commodity derivatives in their characteristics, uses, and markets. For instance, most non-financial derivatives involve a single payment followed by settlement at the end of the contract term, such as a commodity future that sets in advance the price to be paid when products are delivered months later. In contrast, many financial derivatives involve long-term streams of payments between parties, which is more akin to a typical lending relationship.

There is no suggestion that interest rate swaps (the largest category of OTC financial derivatives) or foreign exchange swaps played any role in the financial disruptions of 2008. Yet the House and Senate proposals extend regulatory rules for physical commodities and stocks to these bank-based products. Wantonly extending commodity-focused regulation to financial derivatives applies the wrong tool in the wrong application. The result would be ineffective regulation damaging everything involved. For instance, commodity and stock futures are normally settled by physical delivery whereas most financial derivatives are settled by cash payments—often over an extended period.

Is "Comprehensive" Regulation Appropriate or Necessary?

Gensler is anxious to impose a clearing mandate, among other rules, on OTC derivatives. The mandate would require most derivative contracts to be settled through a clearinghouse rather than directly between the parties. The clearinghouse acts as a middleman, receiving and distributing payments after a contract is formed between the original parties. This arrangement arguably reduces the risk that a contract will not be honored.

What percentage of OTC derivatives contracts can be cleared, at what cost, is critical to determining whether a clearing mandate is appropriate. Gensler asserts that 75 percent of OTC derivatives could be centrally cleared. Gensler's source, however, is not an analysis by his agency, a peer-reviewed study, or a market survey. The only evidence Gensler cites is a ballpark estimate by a single executive whom Gensler never names.[6]

An agency head owes Congress and the public more than an uncorroborated opinion from an unnamed source to justify a massive expansion of regulatory authority. Gensler has not bothered to address this question rigorously, but he has made up his mind and is eager to issue orders to the market.

Gensler and other Obama Administration officials also insist that exemptions to derivatives rules be very narrow. For instance, the Senate Banking Committee bill requires approval from both the principal regulatory agency and certification by the Financial Stability Oversight Council to exempt any end user, swap dealer, bank, non-bank financial institution, security, or other product from derivatives rules. Imposing a duplicative exemption process guarantees that one-size-fits-all mandates will be imposed with little reason.

Uniformity: At What Cost? For What Purpose?

The principal justification for regulating derivatives is that they pose "systemic risks" to the financial system. Yet some derivatives, such as interest rate swaps, pose no systemic risk because their values change slowly and their characteristics are well understood. Other derivative types or user categories are so small as to be insignificant to the overall financial system. Gensler acknowledges, for instance, that corporate end users represent only about 9 percent of derivatives transactions, but he argues against their exemption from collateral requirements for no better reason than to uphold the "regulate everything" principle.[7]

Applying ill-designed blanket regulation will make financial derivatives more costly, more difficult to customize, and consequently less widely used. Because properly used derivatives reduce rather than increase financial risks, bad regulation will increase rather than reduce overall risk in the economy.

"Do Something, Anything"

The Obama Administration and committees in Congress propose to regulate financial derivatives with an antiquated scheme designed for physical commodities. This inflexible and damaging mandate is unjustified. Instead, Congress should:

- Consider carefully any evidence that particular types of derivatives caused or intensified the financial crisis;

- Craft regulations to address specific problems rather than imposing blanket mandates; and
- Create rules that encourage rather than discourage risk-mitigating uses of financial derivatives.

Leading derivatives reform proposals amount to little more than a frenzied insistence to do something, anything, to regulate financial derivatives. Proponents must show why particular derivatives need to be more closely regulated and that the schemes they propose will reduce rather than increase risks in financial markets. if legislation were judged on length and complexity then the Dodd-Frank Act, passed in the wake of the last financial crisis, would constitute an unambiguous triumph.

Alas, the correlation tends to run in the opposite direction. The US Bill of Rights, that most influential and long-standing of modern constitutional documents, fits within a page of A4. The post-2008 financial law, by contrast, is 849 pages long and estimated to have introduced 27,278 new regulatory restrictions.
Just eight years after its passage, Dodd-Frank is unravelling. Gone are the days when the Democrats held the White House and both chambers of Congress — and when, buttressed by public ire following the 2008 bailouts, they were able to pass the most sweeping piece of financial legislation since the Great Depression. President Obama then proclaimed confidently that "this reform will help foster innovation, not hamper it... unless your business model depends on cutting corners or bilking your customers, you've got nothing to fear from reform."

Dodd-Frank, in fact, seems to have accelerated the

decline of small U.S. banks by indiscriminately piling new

regulatory restrictions on them.
But Dodd-Frank did much more than attempt to curtail bad practices. It eliminated previous regulatory agencies and added a slew of new ones. It established a fresh regime for banks deemed of systemic importance. The law also

altered mortgage lending rules, seeking to better reflect the risk of these loans on bank balance sheets. It introduced new regulations on consumer lending, including a cap on debit card fees. It mandated the registration of hedge funds and required added disclosures for traded securities.

Dodd-Frank was a technocrat's dream in its breadth and scope. No crisis-era stone was left unturned, and a great many other future contingencies were addressed.

But the results have been disappointing. A decade after the downturn began, America's biggest financial institutions are larger than ever, accounting for 44 per cent of all bank assets. Dodd-Frank, in fact, seems to have accelerated the decline of small U.S. banks by indiscriminately piling new regulatory restrictions on them. Bank entry, in particular, has ground to a halt, with new bank charters falling from 100 a year pre-crisis to only six in the entire post-crash period. In the meantime, 1,917 incumbent banks have disappeared as a result of merger or failure.

High market concentration, on its own, is neither good nor bad. Bigger banks are better able to diversify and take advantage of scale economies. Moreover, there is reason to believe that America has historically had too many, not too few, banks as a result of state-level restrictions on branching. The above figures, on their own, are thus insufficient to determine whether recent trends have been beneficent or deleterious.

But other evidence suggests that Dodd-Frank has had adverse consequences. Banks, especially small ones, report having discontinued key consumer offerings such as residential mortgages and home equity credit. Technology-enabled lenders have emerged to meet the gap, but only done so partly. Small business credit, half of which is accounted for by the community banks, remains below pre-crisis levels. Worryingly, the evidence suggests that the decline in business lending had a negative and persistent impact on local employment and wages in US counties.

Finally, the rate of unbanked and underbanked households rose in the wake of the crash and has only sluggishly fallen recently. Some 7 per cent of American households presently lack even one bank account, while another 20 per cent rely on (often higher-cost) alternative financial services providers. Unsurprisingly, they cite a too-low average account balance, high fees and a paucity of desirable products as reasons for not banking more. Dodd-Frank is increasingly viewed as an obstacle to, rather than an enabler of, financial well-being and economic growth. Even Barney Frank, the Democrat who co-sponsored the law, has publicly stated that the $50 billion threshold above which financial institutions are deemed systemically important is too low. Indeed, efforts in Congress to lighten the regulatory burden bit by bit have so far been a matter of bipartisan agreement. Only anti-finance firebrands such as Elizabeth Warren remain fiercely opposed to change.

Warren's name is indelibly linked to the Consumer Financial Protection Bureau, arguably the most aggressive of all Obama-era financial regulators. But even at the CFPB, winds of change are blowing. Under Warren's disciple Richard Cordray, the Bureau viewed itself as punisher of financial providers. His Trump-appointed replacement, by contrast, has promised "humility and prudence," and a greater emphasis on cost-benefit analysis. "If a company closes its doors under the weight of [regulation], we still have jobs at CFPB. But what about the workers who are laid off as a result?"

The conventional wisdom, in America as elsewhere, is that pre-2008 financial institutions operated in an unregulated Wild West where consumers were routinely fleeced. In fact, finance has been one of America's most heavily regimented sectors since at least the 1930s. But regulation has often put financial products outside the reach of many households, without the promised benefits of greater safety and soundness. The change of approach touted by the Trump administration is long overdue — let's hope that it materialises.

Contrary to conventional Twitter wisdom, the Economic

Growth, Regulatory Relief, and Consumer Protection Act is

far better news for Main Street than Wall Street. Passed by the House yesterday, the law, derided by critics as the #BankLobbyistAct, would in fact reduce regulatory pressures on small banks, enhance economic mobility, and reduce inequality.

The Dodd-Frank Act was introduced after the financial crisis with the noble intention of protecting consumers and maintaining the stability of the financial system. Unfortunately, a side effect of Dodd-Frank is that the same regulatory stick used on "Too Big to Fail" banks has been punishing community banks, local banks with less than $10 billion in assets. Community banks did not engage in widespread subprime lending or securitization, nor did they engage in risky speculation with derivatives. Their reward? The onerous requirement of complying by the same standards as the big banks.

Community banks are important because they are a vital source of small business funding and are critical to the economic mobility of poorer and rural Americans. The FDIC reported that community banks serve more than

1,200 US counties, including 16.3 million people "who would have limited physical access to mainstream banking services without the presence of community banks." Economic mobility in rural America is poor: Over 85 percent of persistent-poverty counties in the United States are rural. Facing a lack of access to the same services as urban Americans, many rural Americans find it difficult to escape the cycle of poverty. One key tool to beat this is better access to credit, a service provided by well-functioning community banks. That's why it's so worrying to see these banks in decline.

Big banks are increasingly serving only the wealthiest of customers, and are much less connected with local communities than community banks. One of the primary advantages of these localized institutions is their specialized knowledge of their communities. This allows them to make loans to small businesses and individuals who don't fit neatly into the one-size-fits-all financial models of the big banks. Unfortunately, Dodd-Frank was constructed without regard for these relationships.

Regulatory costs are also disproportionate for smaller banks. Small banks cannot spread regulatory costs over a large portfolio of loans, and they lack the ability to hire armies of legal staff to interpret complex, changing requirements. This means community bank boards are forced to become more focused on regulation than serving their customers. For example, instead of hiring an employee to structure products for aspiring entrepreneurs, banks may be forced to hire a compliance officer. These extra costs also leave banks less capable of offering basic banking services to these communities.

Not only does this lead to poorer economic mobility, it also gives larger financial institutions a competitive advantage, contributing further to the concentration of the industry. Unsurprisingly, large financial institutions don't want this to change.

The good news is that yesterday's reforms can provide some positive regulatory relief for smaller banks.

Dodd-Frank originally set the size at which banks will be subject to more stringent regulations at $50 billion in assets. This is far too low. Even Democratic Senator Barney Frank, for whom half the bill is named, publicly supported a higher threshold, believing it would provide a more competitive environment, lessening the dominance of the "mega banks." This reform raises the threshold to $250 billion (with an important caveat), and simply exempts smaller banks from unnecessary and overbearing oversight.

Another great concept is the "regulatory off-ramp." It allows community banks, with assets below $10 billion, an exemption from complicated capital requirements if they satisfy an acceptable level of leverage. In other words, if they take steps to mitigate risk, they are rewarded by exemption from costly requirements.

The so-called #BankLobbyistAct provides modest reforms tailored to community banks. Far from a gift to Wall Street, the bill delivers much-needed relief to Main Street by allowing smaller, more community-focused banks to thrive.

even though the community banks' share of financial assets was already decreasing during the past twenty years, "since the second quarter of 2010—around the time of the passage of the Dodd-Frank Act—their share of U.S. commercial banking assets has declined at a rate almost double that between the second quarters of 2006 and 2010."

The researchers also claim that some of the worst provisions for community banks were those directed specifically at Wall Street. One example is the Volcker Rule, a section of the Dodd-Frank act proposed by former Fed Chairman Paul Volcker that prohibits banks from making certain types of investments The study says this regulation has caused some community banks to sell off assets.

Jim Purcell, president of the State National Bank of Big Spring (Texas), has experienced first-hand the problems community banks are having. His bank is co-plaintiff in a constitutional challenge to Dodd-Frank.

"Dodd-Frank systematically favors big banks over community banks, and that bias poses a serious threat to the banking relationships that community banks, Main Street businesses and other folks have fostered for a century," Purcell said.

He was not very complimentary of the Consumer Financial Protection Bureau (CFPB).

"Dodd-Frank imposes immense regulatory costs upon community banks, costs that are exacerbated by the CFPB's persistently, inherently regulatory uncertainty," Purcell said. "As the CFPB's own web site shows, its rulemakings are the subject of constant, significant revision -- and that's when the CFPB bothers with express rulemakings at all, instead of regulating informally through case-by-case 'guidance' and enforcement proceedings."

The regulations imposed by Dodd-Frank most stifle the little guy. Purcell elaborated that knowing the specifics about the rules as well as how and when to apply them takes significant training, which costs time and money. Ultimately, his bank incurs tens of thousands of dollars in new compliance costs, as a result of the CFPB's "new, unaccountable, and un-transparent regulatory regime." These have an adverse effect on the types of lending activities and other financial services in which community banks like his engage.

"So many requests that our bank and other community banks receive from customers simply don't fit with the big banks' impersonal, automatic approaches," he said. "Community banks like ours know our customers -- we see them every day. And we want our customers to succeed -- they are our community. The big Wall Street banks simply don't have that kind of relationship with American communities."

A longtime Dodd-Frank critic is John Berlau, a senior fellow and an economist with the Competitive Enterprise Institute. He predicted that Dodd-Frank would have a disproportionately deleterious effect on smaller banks. The day President Obama signed the bill, July 15, 2010, he wrote in an article that while aiming to crack down on Wall Street's excesses the harshest impact will be on average businesses that did not cause the crisis.

He feels vindicated after receiving much scorn by many in the media and many politicians who claimed that it will only hurt Wall Street. These same people are starting to see the light.

"Many Democrats and Republicans recognize that Dodd-Frank has had unforeseen negative consequences for community banks and credit unions," he said. "Several bipartisan bills to provide relief to smaller financial institutions have passed the House in the last couple years."

Berlau lamented the fact that former Senate Majority Leader Harry Reid (D-Nev.) never even brought the bills to the floor for a vote.

"Now this will change, and President Obama will have the opportunity to show that he meant what he has said about bipartisanship by signing this relief into law," Berlau said.

Berlau highlighted the one politician adamant about keeping Dodd-Frank the way it is.

"Elizabeth Warren [D-Mass.] seems to be the only person in the country who thinks Dodd-Frank isn't harming community banks," he added.

The report's assessment of Federal Deposit Insurance Corporation data indicated that community banks service a disproportionately large proportion of key segments of the commercial bank lending market – e.g. agricultural, residential mortgage, and small business loans. Particularly troubling to them was the community banks' declining market share in several key lending markets such as the small business market. The study cautions that community banks play an important role in these areas. Even though community banks weathered the financial crisis, since Dodd-Frank Act market share lost is accelerating.

Lux and Greene from the Harvard study suggest that while consolidation in and of itself is not bad, a critical component of the banking sector "may be withering for the wrong reasons." One way to correct this is to revamp federal regulators' cost- benefit analysis and enable regulators to achieve intended goals more efficiently and at lower costs to community banks.

Finally, they say Congress should act to improve existing regulatory processes by and "to establish a bipartisan commission aimed at streamlining existing financial regulations."

www.ingramcontent.com/pod-product-compliance
Lightning Source LLC
Chambersburg PA
CBHW032016170526
45157CB00002B/720

* 9 7 8 1 0 9 6 3 0 1 7 9 0 *